Developing Individual Skills

for the High School Band

Developing Individual Skills for the High School Band

RICHARD WEERTS

parker publishing co., inc.   west nyack, n.y.

For Joan, Larry, Lynn, and Andy

Acknowledgments

The author is indebted to numerous fine instrumentalists and instrumental music teachers who generously offered helpful comments and advice in the preparation of this book. He is grateful to friends and colleagues for their help and encouragement. A special indebtedness is to the people who graciously consented to pose for the photographs. They include Professor Roger E. Cody (trombone, baritone, and tuba), Professor Harold L. Copenhaver (French horn), Professor Lewis S. Danfelt (oboe and bassoon), Anthony DiGrazia (saxophone), Laura George (flute), Ricky George (clarinet), Jeff Piper (trumpet), and Robert Simiele (percussion).

The professional expertise of photographer John A. Kenney is deeply appreciated as are the drawings by artist David Karel. Finally, the author is particularly grateful to Professor Roger Cody and Mr. Robert Simiele for their valuable comments and suggestions regarding the chapters of the book which deal with the brass instruments and the percussion instruments respectively.

The Purpose
of This Book

High school band programs all over the United States are developing rapidly both in quality and quantity. Probably never before in our nation's history have high school bands been at their present level of excellence. Clearly, it is also true that more students are now being reached by school instrumental music programs. All of this rapid growth has placed heavy responsibility on the instrumental music teachers and particularly on the high school band director.

The purpose of this book, therefore, is to aid the band director and instrumental music teacher with the playing and pedagogical problems of the instruments of the band. While this book was written to function in a practical way, it also provides an abundance of reference material for those who are interested in pursuing specific problems more deeply. A number of relevant topics are treated; such as, the importance of small ensembles in developing individual skills, developing effective ways of instrumental practice, the problem of memorizing music, the art of musical interpretation, and the problem of continuing professional growth on the part of the teacher.

This book is designed to serve as a ready reference source—a compendium of useful knowledge for the high school band director. Suggested and graded instructional materials are listed for all of the principal band instruments and various sections treat performance problems which are peculiar to the individual instruments. Photographs and drawings illustrating the text are found throughout the book. Each chapter dealing with the instruments contains an annotated list of solo literature for the instrument discussed. Particular attention is given to the specific individual skills which each solo can be expected to develop. The instrumental chapters also contain selected bibliographies which the teacher can use to pursue individual problems in depth.

Graded literature for numerous and varying small ensemble combinations is included and the bibliography at the conclusion of the book contains an extensive list of books in the area of instrumental music under the headings: General, Clarinet and Saxophone, Oboe, Bassoon, Flute, Reeds, Acoustics, Trumpet, French Horn, Trombone and Baritone, Tuba, Percussion, and Encyclopedias and Dictionaries which might be of interest and use to the instrumental music teacher.

This book, then, should be a valuable aid to the high school band director interested in developing the individual skills of his students while still working within the context and framework of his normal educational setting.

Contents

Chapter 11, The Trumpet (*Cont*)

Chapter 12, The French Horn • 139

Chapter 13, The Trombone • 155

Chapter 14, The Baritone • 169

Chapter 15, The Tuba • 180

Developing Individual Skills
for the High School Band

I

TEACHING SKILLS FOR INDIVIDUAL DEVELOPMENT

CHAPTER 1

How to Teach the Art of
Individual Musical Interpretation

The art of musical interpretation is indeed a complex and intricate one. Yet, in many cases, it is interpretation that separates a good musical performance from a superb one—an artist from a fine technician. It is entirely possible for a musician (or musical organization) to perform in tune, with good tone quality, play everything on the printed page, and yet sound banal, bland, and uninspiring. As H. A. Vandercook states:

> However, even if he follows these plainly marked directions to the letter, the performer will still find a great deal lacking in his rendition of the passage, especially so after he has heard an experienced and artistic musician interpret it.[1]

The art of musical interpretation is difficult to explain verbally and perhaps equally difficult to comprehend. Clearly, it is what makes music an art and not merely a routine mechanical science.

Adapting musical interpretation to individual talents

Ivan Galamian terms interpretation "the final goal of all instrumental study, its only *raison d'etre.*"[2] Teaching according to rigid

---

[1]H. A. Vandercook, *Expression in Music* (Chicago: Rubank, Inc., Revised edition, 1942), p. 1.

[2]Ivan Galamian, *Principles of Violin Playing and Teaching* (Englewood Cliffs, N.J.: Prentice-Hall, Inc., 1962), p. 62.

and inflexible rules, using the same material for every student, and demanding that the student attempt to emulate one "correct" interpretation are all open to a great deal of question. The material used in teaching must be adapted to the individual needs of each student. The student must understand the meaning of the music thoroughly. He must have creative imagination and a personal-emotional approach to the work if his performance is to be lifted above the dry and the pedantic.[3]

Too many teachers tend to be rigid and dogmatic when the question of interpretation arises. Most appear to be firmly convinced of the correctness of their interpretative ideas and seem to have little or no sympathy with other interpretations. However, the possibility of many widely differing yet very acceptable musical intepretations has been brought out by a number of eminent authorities. Aaron Copland has pointed out:

> A composition is, after all, an organism. It is a living, not a static, thing. That is why it is capable of being seen in a different light and from different angles by various interpreters or even by the same interpreter at different times.[4]

Donald Ferguson suggests:

> While a given figure may have an elemental or intrinsic value of suggestion, the possibility of appropriate musical variation is as great as the variety of mood that demands expression.[5]

James Mursell comments:

> It is very valuable for a mature artist to hear how other performers deal with a work he himself is studying, even though he may not follow their interpretation.[6]

Mathis Lussy states:

> The pupil will emancipate himself by gaining a knowledge

---

[3]*Ibid.*

[4]Aaron Copland, *What to Listen for in Music* (New York: McGraw-Hill Book Co., Inc., 1939), p. 247.

[5]Donald N. Ferguson, *On the Elements of Musical Expression* (Minneapolis: University of Minnesota, 1944), p. 61.

[6]James L. Mursell, *Music Education* (New York: Silver Burdett Co., 1956), p. 284.

of the notes which generate expression, and of the modes of execution adopted by the great artists to express their sensations. He will no longer depend solely and blindly on the sentiment of his master, but on his own, enlightened by reason and study, and will discover for himself how to give life and poetry to the works which he executes.[7]

Other performers and teachers rely entirely on the *notation* as the ultimate guide and final authority for the correct interpretation. Mursell points out, however:

Although the constant tendency of notation is to indicate more and more the composer's intention, it can only feature the high points of the musical structure. The notation can only give the performer certain cues. To make a proper use of these cues, he must rely on his musical understanding.[8]

Gomer Pound states:

Our system of notation is adequate only to a degree. Beyond a certain point it is a matter of artistic interpretation on the part of the performer.[9]

Vandercook points out that: "At best, a page of music may be considered as a blueprint of the plans and specifications of the melody and the manner in which it is to be played."[10]

Thus, the study of interpretation should broaden and extend the student's musical understanding and present him with some ideas to aid in the development or alteration of his own interpretation. Mursell has stated: "Instead of slavish copying there should be musical understanding, and along with that, some initiative in interpretation."[11]

Ways to develop interpretation

It becomes apparent that musical interpretation is clearly a developmental process that accrues over a period of time. Moreover, one's interpretation should never become fixed and static.

---

[7]Mathis Lussy, *Musical Expression*, Tr. by M. E. Von Glehn (London: H. W. Gray Co., 1915), pp. 11–12.

[8]Mursell, p. 157.

[9]Gomer Pound, "Variety in Tone Color," *The Clarinet*, Vol. 20, Autumn, 1955, p. 9.

[10]VanderCook, p. 1.

[11]Mursell, p. 286.

There must be room for musical growth and change in musical expression. The mature artist is continually seeking to alter (usually minutely and imperceptibly) his interpretations of the compositions he studies and performs.

One of the best ways to develop the highly creative process of musical interpretation is through extensive, intensive, continual, and intelligent *listening* to fine performances. There is no substitute for hearing and studying fine "live" performances. Where this is not possible fine recordings can be of great help.

Performing alongside a fine musician in a chamber group or orchestra can be a valuable source of help and inspiration. When possible (and when one is available), studying with an artist *teacher-performer* is another excellent approach to the development of interpretation. Perhaps it should be emphasized that the musician must have a good technical command of his medium of musical expression whether this be voice, clarinet, violin, band, or orchestra. The better technical facility he possesses the freer he will be to concentrate on musical expression. In a like manner, the better the performer knows the printed notation the more released he will be to think of expressing it in an artistic and musical way.

The value of studying different interpretations

The value of studying many diverse interpretations would not seem to be fully realized by considering any as models to be imitated or even emulated. Nor would there appear to be much worth in merely labeling certain interpretations as "inferior" and others as "superior." It is inferred that, to make this kind of study a *learning* experience leading toward maximum *musical growth*, one must consider the different interpretations as aids in developing clear and lucid perceptions of the compositions as pieces of music. It seems reasonable to conclude that once a thorough musical comprehension has been achieved the individual can be expected (and indeed encouraged) to develop his own interpretation. Again, however, it is emphasized that individuals should have acquired the necessary preliminary musical and technical development to commence at this level of study.

Another value which accrues from the intensive study of many dissimilar musical performances is the development of a genuine appreciation of and respect for other musicians' modes of musical expression. An unbiased, objective approach to such a study is essential in order for the greatest possible musical development to take place.

In many interpretations a student might find a genuine and intriguing musical goal for which to strive. An experienced performer may well approach the expression of a composition in a completely new and different light as a result of insights gained from the study of several contrasting renditions of the work. The teacher can use the widely differing recorded performances to point out the vast number of possibilities and variations in appropriate musical expression as he guides and encourages his students in the development of their distinctive styles.

It can also be concluded that notation, per se, should not be viewed as the sole guide and terminal authority in developing an interpretation. Notation plays an important role and should be a useful guide, but artistic expression can better evolve through musical understanding and insight gained from a knowledge of many interpretations.

Clearly, the nebulous art of musical interpretation should be pursued in a systematic and well-planned manner by all serious musicians and students of music. It is the soul of musical performance.[12]

---

[12]Richard Weerts, "The Nebulous Art of Musical Interpretation," *The American Music Teacher*, January-February, 1965, p. 26 & 34. © 1965 MTNA, Inc. Used by permission.

CHAPTER 2

How to Develop Effective Ways
of Individual Instrumental
Practice

Professor Ruth Strang has said that "the pupil is the center of ever-widening circles of influence."[1] It is readily apparent to the instrumental director that the ever-increasing myriad of activities of modern day living and full academic schedules compete keenly for the student's time. The era is past when instrumental music students could practice three and four hours a day. Actually, the instrumental student of today usually has a limited amount of time available for practice. Unfortunate also is the probability that a great deal of the practicing does not achieve the optimum results it should.

Most teachers and students are aware of the familiar exhortations regarding practicing; that is, daily practice, practicing at approximately the same time every day, and following certain procedures recommended by the teacher. These, of course, are good advice as far as they go. It would seem, however, that many of the problems lie in how the student uses this daily time set aside for practice.

---

[1]Ruth Strang, "Guidance: Its Larger Responsibilities," *Teachers College Record*, Vol. 56, No. 7, April, 1955, p. 370.

Mechanical practice versus intelligent practice

Poor methods of practice can indeed do a student more harm than good. Galamian states:

> It happens only too often with too many students that the mind wanders to different spheres while the fingers and hands are engaged in mechanical routine-functioning and endless repetition. Practice of this kind, lacking both direction and control, is a waste of time and effort. Not only does it not achieve what it sets out to do, but also it can sometimes be positively harmful. Mistakes are repeated over and over again, and the ear becomes impervious to faulty sounds.[2]

Ernest Bayles declares: "It is not how many times a thing is done that counts. It is the grasp the learner has of it that makes the difference." He continues: "We need to get completely away from repetitive drill. Whenever repetitive drill is invoked, learning will suffer."[3]

The road to the mastery of any instrument is long and arduous at best and much application and perseverance are required of every instrumental music student. It is true that talent helps to make the way easier than it otherwise would be, but even talent cannot be substituted for the hard work of intelligent practicing. Perhaps it should be made clear at this point that a case is not being made for less practice. However, much better musical results can be achieved through thoughtful and intelligent use of what practice time one does have. It is obvious that some students get less from three hours of practicing than a more analytical player may get from one hour of concentrated practice toward clearly defined and understood objectives. One of the most important things a teacher should instill in his students is the ability to practice intelligently and to use practice time wisely. It would seem absolutely essential that he show his students how to practice and what to practice for.

---

[2]Ivan Galamian, *Principles of Violin Playing and Teaching* (Englewood Cliffs, N.J.: Prentice-Hall, Inc., 1962), p. 94.

[3]Ernest E. Bayles, "The Idea of Learning as Development of Insight." Reprinted in *Readings for Educational Psychology* (New York: Thomas Y. Crowell Co., 1958), p. 40.

Using the daily practice period in developing individual skills

When one thinks in terms of efficient and effective instrumental practice, the first area of consideration logically turns to the "warm-up" period. A tenable way to warm up, both physically and mentally, is by playing long tones, lip slurs, interval slurs, and similar exercises. There is an unfortunate tendency to make this portion of the practice period routine and perfunctory. If this is the case, the best results will certainly not be achieved. Again, the mind must be actively engaged and the student must be aware of what goals he is trying to achieve. (In the case of reed players, it should be pointed out that trying-out and adjusting reeds should not be construed to be a part of the practice period. Clearly, this process is essential, but it should be done at other times.)

Practicing Long Tones. There are numerous variations that can be employed to make the practicing of long tones both interesting and beneficial. For example, some long tones should be played in all of the registers of the instrument. Moreover, long tones should be practiced at all levels of volume, from *pianissimo* through *fortissimo*. Here breath control and deep diaphragmatic breathing need to be considered. The long tones should not be played so softly that they do not have an element of substance about them or so loudly that they become distorted and out of control. Yet another variation is the procedure of starting the tone softly, developing a crescendo, and following this with a diminuendo.

In the case of interval slurs, a number of different intervals should be practiced—not merely the usual fifths and octaves. As the long tones and interval slurs are practiced the student should develop the art of concentrating on such aspects of his tone as quality, color, timbre, and intonation. Unless the student has perfect pitch it is helpful to refer to an electronic tuning device for guidance regarding intonation. It is an interesting psychological phenomenon that the ear can be deceived regarding intonation; that is, if the ear hears a note slightly out of tune, this out of tune note will, over a period of time, tend to sound in tune. Of a one-and-a-half hour practice period a minimum of eight to ten minutes should be assigned to the practice and study of long tones, interval slurs, and related exercises.

Practicing Scales. The next item in a sequential pattern of the daily practice period could well be the practice of scales (major and minor), scales in thirds, arpeggios, the inversion of arpeggios, and various related fundamentals hereafter referred to in the interest of brevity as the "scale family." (Other closely related fundamental exercises might include the major, minor, diminished seventh, augmented circles, whole tone scales, and the circle of dominant sevenths.) This activity is disliked by many students for a number of reasons. The scale family is regarded by many as dry, dull, and genuinely uninteresting. Furthermore, many students cannot see the value to be gained from the practice of such exercises. As a result of these negative attitudes, many students either fail to practice the scale family entirely or do so in such a lackadaisical fashion as to derive little or no benefit from such practice.

As any skilled musician will readily attest, a thorough knowledge of the scale family (developed over a period of time) is essential to the musician's training and development. A thorough knowledge of these fundamental exercises is bound to increase the student's technical command of his instrument. As a result, more and better musical literature will come within his ability to study and perform. A thorough knowledge of the scale family should also increase and enhance the student's sight-reading ability. Clearly, these fundamentals should be committed to memory at an early date.

A number of interesting and valuable variations in the practice of the scale family are available to the student. For example, they can be practiced at widely differing tempi—sometimes slowly, sometimes quite rapidly, but always under control and with good intonation and tone quality. The student should practice the scale family both slurred and tongued, as well as with various articulative devices. The tonguing of these exercises, at numerous tempi, is a good way to develop fine coordination between tongue and fingers—an aspect of performance so necessary to a good technical command of the instrument. Various styles of tonguing can also be employed; such as, legato, portato, and staccato. A common problem which the student must constantly be aware of is that the level of tone quality tends to drop during the execution of tongued exercises and passages. The maintenance of a good embouchure during the playing of tongued passages will help to prevent this. Various articulative devices should be injected into the practicing of the scale family. These might include the following:

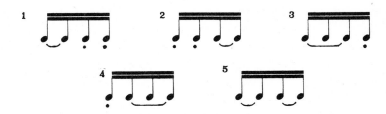

Using a Metronome. It is also very good practice to use an electric metronome from time to time while playing scales and technical études. It is quite possible, even for an advanced performer, to think that such exercises are being played with accuracy and precision when, in fact, this may not be the case. An electric metronome will help to instill greater accuracy in one's playing of the scale family and technical exercises. Another closely related benefit that should accrue from working with the metronome is the valuable ability to ascertain different tempi with a degree of accuracy when no metronome is readily available.

The argument that the metronome will make one's playing too "mechanical" is largely fallacious. There is a far greater tendency for the student's playing to lack precision and accuracy because of little or no practice with a metronome. Approximately 15 minutes should be allotted to the practice of the scale family during the daily practice period.

Following the practice of the scale family the student could logically turn to his étude material. The assigned étude material varies widely. It could include a number of less difficult études or only one of advanced difficulty. An area where many students are noticeably weak in the study of étude material is that of *rhythm*. A better result will probably be achieved if the student is taught to *feel* rhythm through the slight tapping of his foot. He should also be taught to subdivide the beat when counting rhythm; that is, an étude in common time should be counted one *and* two *and* three *and* four *and*, as opposed to merely counting one-two-three-four. In compound time, such as a march written in six-eight rhythm, the student should subdivide in terms of six beats while actually counting two beats per bar. These procedures will produce much greater accuracy in the area of rhythm.

The student should, moreover, be able to explain precisely where any given note in a measure falls, and he should be able to demonstrate this on his instrument. A great deal of time, effort, and frustration can often be saved by solving the rhythmic problems in an étude *before* trying to perform it on the instrument. In the case of a particularly perplexing rhythmic passage, one can break the component rhythmic parts down to their lowest common denominator and then proceed to "tap" or "speak" the rhythm before attempting to play it.

Teaching Dynamics. Dynamics often need to be exaggerated by performers. Many times an instrumentalist thinks he is making a definite distinction between a *mezzo-forte* and *forte* passage when actually there is virtually no difference at all. Playing at essentially one level of volume is a common malady. The key word in the execution of most crescendos and diminuendos is *gradual.* This, too, is not always accomplished and yet it is an important aspect of musical interpretation. A high quality tape recorder can be of great value in the study of one's overall performance—its use is highly recommended.

In terms of the slow, lyrical études, the student must be cognizant of such aspects of musical performance as phrasing, tone quality, intonation, and interpretation. In the case of the more rapid, technical études attention must be given to accuracy, smoothness, and precision in addition to beauty of tone and good intonation. As indicated previously, it is wise to employ an electric metronome during the practice of technical études and technical passages in solo literature. It is also good practice to be able to play rapid, technical études at different speeds—some slow, some fast. It is even salutary *occasionally* to play a technical étude at a tempo beyond which it can be handled well. If this is done extensively, however, it will tend to develop poor playing habits lacking in both precision and accuracy.

At least once during each practice period the student should play his étude and solo material from beginning to end without stopping for any reason. This will help him to achieve a clearer picture of the material as a whole and is a valid procedure both psychologically and pedagogically. This procedure, however, cannot be done in excess without the development of undesirable playing habits. A minimum of 30 minutes is suggested for the practice of étude material.

Another important area with which every serious secondary student needs to become acquainted is that of fine solo literature for his instrument. Clearly, much of what has been said regarding the practice of étude material will also be applicable to the study of solo literature. It is also helpful to have the services of a skilled accompanist available even if public performances are not anticipated. This would seem to be particularly important in the study of sonata and sonata-style literature, as well as nearly all contemporary solo literature. A minimum of 20 to 25 minutes could wisely be assigned to this area of study.

Practicing Sight-Reading. No practice period should be considered complete without some work in the area of sight-reading. Being skilled at sight-reading is certainly one of the differences between an outstanding performer and a merely good performer. This valuable skill can, to a great degree, be acquired by sight-reading extensively over a long period of time. The material chosen for this purpose is of considerable importance. It should be neither so easy as to be of little or no value to the student nor so difficult as to be virtually impossible for the student to read with any degree of accuracy. During this period the student should not attempt to "practice" the music intended for sight-reading purposes. Rather, he should take a few minutes to look over the material and then proceed to read through it with the idea of stopping as few times as possible. Sight-reading need not be discouraging if the material is carefully chosen by the student's teacher. A minimum of ten minutes daily should be assigned to this area.

It should be made clear at this point that there is no substitute for private lessons from the best specialist available. The skilled teacher-performer is indeed indispensable to the training and development of the instrumentalist. The best results will be achieved if the private teacher possesses expertise in at least two areas; that is, he must have pedagogical skill, and he should be able to perform in a quasi-professional manner on the instrument(s) he teaches. It is also essential that he be in sympathy with the instrumental music director and school instrumental music program. There should be a feeling of rapport and mutual understanding between the school instrumental music director and the private studio teacher. This is important if the best interests of the student are to be served.

Clearly, the preceding description of the daily practice period could (and indeed should) vary with individual students. The specific content of the practice period should always be open to review and possible revision by both the student and his teacher working in conjunction in order to achieve the best results.

Correcting common fallacies regarding practice

Many believe that practicing is the formation of "habits" which, hopefully, will improve their performances. Concerning this, Mursell states cogently that, "the formation of a habit is a symptom of satisfaction; and when habits form, learning and improvement stop."[4] Habit should, therefore, be considered as a stopping place, a point of satisfaction. To a large extent improvement depends upon *breaking*, not forming habits.

"Practice makes perfect" is a widely accepted cliché. It should be noted that practice with little or no understanding will approach perfection at a slow pace and, in fact, may never reach it. On the other hand, there would seem to be considerable truth in saying that the less the practice the better will be the learning, as long as the reduction of practice depends upon the deepening, strengthening, and clarifying of understanding.[5]

A common belief is that it is possible to learn only while practicing; that is, during the actual practice period. Actually, much improvement can accrue in the intervals *between* practice sessions. Indeed, it is quite possible that some of the best practicing one does can occur without making a sound. Mursell has stated that, "it is not true to say that we learn only by doing. It is possible to learn a great deal by thinking."[6]

---

[4]James L. Mursell, *Psychology for Modern Education* (New York: W. W. Norton and Company, Inc., 1952), p. 144.

[5]*Ibid.*, p. 154.

[6]*Ibid.*, p. 166.

Eleven keys for improving individual skills during practice time[7]

1. The *will to learn* seems to be of basic importance, for without it all else is of little avail. Intrinsically intertwined within the will to learn is *purpose*, for musical growth depends upon both.
2. The practice period(s) should be reserved specifically for this activity and should be entirely free from interruption and interference.
3. The instrument should be in excellent mechanical condition. An instrument in poor mechanical condition can do much to discourage even an enthusiastic student.
4. The development of confidence is important, for a lack of it has a tendency to block the learning process.
5. Relaxation, or the maximum cancellation of antagonistic pulls, also plays a key role during the practice of a musical instrument. Clearly, muscles should be limber, not tense.
6. Good learning requires the constant application of both intelligence and analysis, for the moment *thinking* stops *learning* stops also.
7. Long continued practice eventually reaches a point of diminishing returns and can produce negative rather than positive results. On the other hand, the distribution of one's practice time to two shorter periods daily would seem to be beneficial.
8. The practicing of a musical instrument requires a great deal of physical energy as well as mental alertness and concentration. Practicing when one is physically and/or mentally enervated tends to produce negative results.
9. The expectation of constant, rapid, and continued improvement is, in most cases, unrealistic. Many times a plateau will be reached when there will be little or no noticeable improvement for quite some time. As a matter of fact, there might very well be occasional periods of

---

[7]Richard Weerts, "The Effective Use of Practice Time with Implications and Recommendations for the Instrumental Music Student," *The Instrumentalist*, January, 1964, pp. 42–43. © 1964 *The Instrumentalist*. Used by permission.

regression or "backsliding." The more advanced an instrumentalist becomes, the slower and less obvious is his apparent or noticeable progress.

10. Learning to hear ourselves as we actually sound to others is of cardinal importance. The instrumentalist can profit greatly by listening to and studying tape recordings of his playing. Movies of one's practicing and performance can provide further insights toward improvement. The ability for honest, objective hearing or the ability to hear the sound as the audience would hear it should be a major goal of practicing.

11. Finally, the development and cultivation of high musical ideals is most significant. Working toward one's musical ideals should be a *lifetime* goal—a goal that is never reached. As the late Fritz Kreisler said of his career: "I have achieved only a medium approach to my ideal in music. I got only fairly near."[7]

---

[8]Fritz Kreisler, quoted in *Time*, Vol. 62, No. 4, February 9, 1962, p. 64.

CHAPTER 3

How to Attack the Problem of Memorizing Music in Developing Individual Skills

Most musicians eventually must come to terms with the problem of memorization. Sooner or later the student, the teacher, and the professional will probably be called upon to memorize music or to provide guidance and instruction in this area. For the concert artist and opera performer extensive memorization is normally mandatory. On the other hand, the memorization requirements for a wind instrument player in a symphony orchestra would, in all probability, be far less extensive. Some competence in the area of memorization, however, is salutary for *all* performing musicians. In the interest of clarification, it should be indicated that it is not the purpose here to pursue the polemics of memorization's role (if indeed one does exist) in "training the mind." This issue is, within the framework of the present discussion, largely incidental.

For the few people who possess a "photographic memory," memorization is obviously no problem. For many, however, it can cause a considerable amount of consternation, anxiety, and frustration. The fact of the matter is that some excellent musicians do experience a great deal of difficulty in memorizing music. Few will contend that the ability to memorize effectively and efficiently is not a valuable asset to any musician. The purpose here is to explore the problem and to offer some practical recommendations.

Correcting common fallacies regarding memorization

Many people accept the popular fallacy that one is either born with or without a good memory. This "either-or" concept leads to futility if the person does not seem to have this innate gift. Mursell states, however, that effective memorization is "an ability that can, to a large extent, be acquired."[1]

He continues:

> To be sure, psychologists usually believe that no one can increase the actual amount of "memory power" with which he was born. But there is no doubt that one can learn to use to good effect this power, of whatever magnitude it may be.[2]

Most authorities concur, however, that there is no quick and easy way to effective memorization. Clearly, apathy and repetition per se will not produce the desired results. On the other hand, it is probably true that many musicians expend considerably more time and effort in memorizing music than should be the case.

Understanding memorization, learning, stage fright, and relaxation

Memorization and learning are very closely related and, in many cases, the two processes are intrinsically intertwined. What makes for effective learning also aids effective memorization. Too many people tend to think of memorization as a mysterious mental trick or a distinctive talent apart from learning. Yet memorization is not a special kind of learning, for it has the same basic characteristics as all learning.[3]

Repetition in Memorization. One of the poorest ways to memorize music is by sheer repetition with little insight or thought. The number of times a composition is played actually makes little difference. It is the ever-increasing growth in the musical and in-

---

[1] James L. Mursell, *Using Your Mind Effectively* (New York: McGraw-Hill Book Company, Inc., 1951), p. 193.

[2] *Ibid.*

[3] James L. Mursell, *Psychology for Modern Education*, p. 228.

tellectual *understanding* of the composition which contributes to thorough memorization. Moreover, we tend to memorize more effectively when we have a specific purpose—a definite challenge, such as performing a solo from memory in public on a certain date. Many authorities in the field of educational psychology indicate that *good organization* is the most important factor, the *sine qua non* in learning for excellent retention. They point out that "one should relate what is to be learned into a coherent structure, or organize it in terms of some integrating principle, so that the individual items are carried, so to speak, by the intrinsic pattern."[4]

Combating Stage Fright. An area closely related to both learning and memorizing music is that of stage fright. The problem of stage fright and its concomitant physiological and psychological ramifications are extensively treated in excellent articles by Anna Y. Martin and Hilmar Wagner.[5] It is not the purpose here to delve into the phenomenon of stage fright except to point out its involvement and relatedness to the problem of producing music from memory in public. Hilmar Wagner points out the interesting fact that "many performers seem to play better when they do not have to concern themselves with the written page or worry about page turning."[6] Professional musicians have long concurred with the philosophy that one of the best ways to guard against stage fright is through the procedure of extensive and thorough preparation. This is, of course, no guarantee against stage fright since no guarantee does, in fact, exist.

How to Relax. How important relaxation can be to instrumental playing is cogently stated by the solo clarinetist of the Boston Symphony Orchestra, Gino Cioffi. Cioffi tells us that, "there is no doubt in my mind whatsoever but that the key to advanced clarinet playing lies in the ability of the player to relax his muscles when playing."[7] If a poll were to be taken it would probably indicate that few teachers indeed have not advised their students to

---

[4]Arthur Gates, Arthur Jersild, T. R. McConnell, Robert C. Challman, *Educational Psychology* (New York: The Macmillan Company, 1950), p. 403.

[5]Anna Y. Martin, "The Physiological and Psychological Concomitants of Stage Freight" *Music Educators Journal* (January, 1964), pp. 100–108. Hilmar Wagner, "Stage Fright" (Part I) *The Instrumentalist*, December, 1963, pp. 36–37; (Part II), January, 1964, pp. 51–52.

[6]*Ibid.* (Part II), p. 51.

[7]Gino B. Cioffi, "On Clarinet Playing," *The Clarinet*, Fall, 1953, p. 11.

relax while playing. Yet how many instrumentalists there are whose throats, jaws, hands, fingers, and even entire bodies seem to tense up the moment they begin to play. It is apparent that few know how to relax, and perhaps even fewer know how to apply relaxation to their playing.

Some teachers treat the problem of relaxation by not discussing it; that is, they feel their students will actually be made *more conscious* of their tenseness if it is discussed with them. Yet it seems more probable that a considerable amount of tenseness can be eliminated if the teacher and student work together in trying to locate the source of the tension and then attempt to find ways to go about reducing it. It should be kept in mind, however, that some tension is necessary in musical performance. As Mursell points out: "The notion of relaxation is very closely associated with that of coordination. It is impossible to have any kind of directed movement and at the same time to maintain complete relaxation."[8]

Although most authorities in the fields of medicine and psychology would probably agree that relaxation is quite important to one's health and general well-being, this art is, for most people, not easy to achieve. The widely known authority in the area of relaxation, Dr. Edmund Jacobson, advocates training and treats the subject extensively in his thought-provoking book, *You Must Relax.*[9] This text is highly recommended for those who wish to pursue deeply the subject of relaxation and its many concomitant ramifications.

The problem of relaxation should be dealt with from the *beginning* of training in instrumental music. The psychological, physiological, and neurological phenomenon of tension is a difficult syndrome to break when the student has reached high school age. Clearly, relaxation in the area of instrument playing should be dealt with at all levels of instrumental study.

What specifically can be done to aid in the process of developing relaxation? Keith Stein concludes: "The ability to recognize relaxation as well as tension and to know how to apply relaxed

---

[8]James L. Mursel, *Psychology of Music* (New York: W. W. Norton and Company, Inc., 1937), p. 46.

[9]Edmund Jacobson, *You Must Relax*, Fourth Edition (New York: McGraw-Hill Book Company, Inc.), 1957.

principles within areas where muscular support is required (as well as to be able to 'let go' in all other areas) is one of the great secrets of playing."[10] A first step then might be the cognizance of both tension and relaxation in one's playing. Both tension and relaxation tend to be contagious. If there is an *awareness* of these two opposites there seems to be a better chance that something positive can be done to achieve the desired results.

Benefits of Relaxing. Developing a relaxed approach to instrumental playing is undoubtedly intertwined with developing a relaxed approach to other areas of life. This obviously cannot be accomplished in merely a few days. On the other hand, much can be done and many beneficial results accrued over an extended period of time. Many excellent ideas can be secured by extensive reading on the subject, and most players will eventually develop their own approaches to solving the problem. Some students will naturally perform in a relaxed manner, but many will need help and guidance in this area. There is an abundance of examples on all levels of development where tension clearly inhibits and blocks the student's progress.

The following are but a few of many methods designed to eliminate or at least reduce tension in instrumental playing. Robert Marcellus, solo clarinetist of the Cleveland Orchestra, explains that, "For me, a five-minute 'breather' every twenty-five or thirty minutes is essential, for it relaxes not only the embouchure, but lessens the mental fatigue, which builds up gradually."[11] Stein suggests that one deliberately attempt to tense up his entire body and then let go all at once.[12] He further recommends "tightening up small areas of the body followed by an immediate relaxation of the same parts."[13] Cioffi recommends slow practice and explains that:

> The entire body should be relaxed; sit or stand properly, don't slouch in your seat or cross your legs. Allow all your muscles to be free, not cramped. Be sure that the arms swing freely from the shoulders, that elbows are free; the wrists so relaxed that the hands droop when the arms are

---

[10]Keith Stein, *The Art of Clarinet Playing* (Evanston: Summy-Birchard Company, 1958), p. 16.

[11]Robert Marcellus, "Relax and Live Longer," *The Clarinet*, Summer, 1952, p. 4.

[12]Keith Stein, p. 16.

[13]Keith Stein, p. 17.

raised. If the wrists and forearms are relaxed the fingers will follow suit.[14]

The development of a relaxed approach to learning, memorization, and instrumental playing in general is indeed both a *related* and an *extended* project. The results in terms of achieving a more complete mastery of the instrument, better learning, and better memorization would seem to be well worth working for.

15 ways to teach improved memorization

1. In order to memorize with the greatest degree of certainty and effectiveness, one should have a *clearly defined goal or purpose*. Actually, the more consciously and purposefully one works toward a future challenging occasion, the more effectively will he probably memorize. It has been found, over a period of time, that students who are willing to accept the challenge and responsibility for memorization requirements and who do, in fact, memorize music *regularly* seem to experience far less difficulty in this area than students who try every possible way to *avoid* memorizing music.

2. It is essential to understand the *entire score* of the composition to be memorized. This implies at least a functional knowledge of its structure, form, and harmonic, as well as melodic, content. Too many students concern themselves with the melodic line and little else.

3. One must be constantly on the *qui vive* since this attitude of skilled alertness is a major factor in effective memorization. Careful attention to detail, as well as a knowledge of the composition as a whole, is important.

4. Memory cannot be developed and strengthened most effectively by repetitious exercise alone. Improvement must evolve from insight and training in the technique of learning.

5. The memory is controllable by suggestion, and recall depends a great deal upon mental attitude. A positive approach to the business of memorization can be very beneficial. Positive suggestion before a public performance can also be helpful.

---

[14]Gino Cioffi, p. 12.

6. The development of confidence is quite essential, for a lack of it has a tendency to inhibit the learning (and thus the memorization) process. On the other hand, an attitude of over-confidence frequently interferes with the efficient and effective memorization of music.

7. Truly effective memorization involves having the music so well memorized that the performer is able to devote the majority of his conscious effort to the job of *interpreting* the work he is performing. He should be at ease so that he feels a rapport with his audience; that is, he should feel that he is truly *communicating*, in a musical way, with his audience.

8. A relaxed approach to the problem of memorization is important since tension has a tendency to block the memorization process.

9. Warming-up is too often merely a physical matter. There should be mental warming-up as well, and the mind needs to be engaged at all times. Practicing without any goal or purpose and with the mind not engaged will, in all probability, reap more in the way of negative results than positive results.

10. Attempting to perform from memory when one is enervated frequently will negate much careful and painstaking preparation. The performer should be as rested as possible before performing from memory in public.

11. Careful *pacing* of one's preparation of a memorized work is important. It is frequently a good procedure to memorize the composition to be performed and then *not* practice it at all for several weeks. When practice is then resumed a more thorough and deeper understanding is often achieved. As a corollary to this premise, it is true that once a composition has been thoroughly memorized (with intellectual insight and musical understanding), it will usually be relatively easy to memorize again—even after a considerable period of time has elapsed.

12. Performing from memory in public as often as possible seems to have a salutary effect on developing the memorization process. This premise is based on the assumption that the performer is well prepared for the public performance. A student who attempts to perform in public

from memory with little or poor preparation does himself a definite disservice. This is not to imply that good preparation insures a good public performance—it does not. It is, however, a necessity if the student seriously intends to develop expertise in the ability to perform music in public from memory.

13. An attitude of perseverance and determination is necessary in the development of the ability to memorize music. Very rarely will progress be rapid and continuous. In many cases there will be periods of discouragement and obvious regression. The performer who has the resilience and drive to continuously and thoughtfully work toward the goal of effective memorization will usually achieve good results.

14. Memorization can also be aided by careful listening (both with and without the score) to recorded performances of the composition. A variation of this procedure is for the performer to make a tape recording of the work to be memorized and then to study the recording. It should be noted that a better effect is usually achieved if the accompaniment is included on the tape recording.

15. Finally, the memorization process is very much a personal and individual matter which must be gradually developed by the individual musician. It is quite possible that what will be an effective procedure for memorizing music for one individual will not be effective at all for another person. It is also quite possible (and indeed salutary) for a musician to alter his method of memorizing as he matures and develops.

The memorization of music may be viewed as an ability that can largely be acquired. While few are born with prodigious memory power, most musicians can learn to make better use of what memory power they do have. No easy, quick method seems to be usually available. Like any other worthwhile task, increasing the effectiveness of one's memory demands a considerable expenditure of time and thoughtful hard work. The results should be rewarding, gratifying, and useful to the instrumental music student.

CHAPTER 4

How to Use Small Ensembles in Developing Individual Skills

It is probably true that few instrumental directors would debate the importance of a strong small ensemble program in their schools. Yet in many cases this program leaves much to be desired in both quality and quantity. In many schools it receives lip-service only. Frequently interested students are left entirely on their own in terms of finding suitable music, assistance with rehearsal techniques, and someone to provide constructive criticism of their work.

When a director is asked the reasons for a lagging small ensemble program, his answers are frequently:

1. There is not enough *time* available, and
2. There is not enough *professional staff* available.

But are these really the reasons? Perhaps a better explanation is offered by Gordon Peters: "It basically boils down to the educator being convinced of the *assets* of such a program before embarking on an *investment* of time, music, and eventually, additional instruments."[1] Peters then lists 26 objectives of a suggested

---

[1] Gordon Peters, "Why Percussion Ensembles?" *The Instrumentalist*, April, 1962, p. 55.

percussion ensemble program.[2] Many of these could apply equally well to any small instrumental ensemble program.

Profiting with the small ensemble program

Perhaps one of the most forceful reasons for the existence of this program is that "the training gained from playing in small ensembles is superior to that in large groups."[3] Clearly, it should be the responsibility of the instrumental director to inaugurate, supervise, and perpetuate numerous small ensemble activities in his school. There can be little doubt that the training and musical growth achieved in a small ensemble will afford beneficial results to the large ensembles.

Beginning Ensembles. It is important to emphasize that small ensemble experience should not be reserved for the intermediate and advanced students only, for *all* students can profit from extensive and varied small ensemble experience. For example, there is no reason why students cannot begin small ensemble experience after only a few months of instrumental study. Certainly this experience should be started no later than after the first year. Within the public school setting small ensemble experience should be well planned and continuous through the 12th grade. Indeed, numerous successful band directors have *required* all members of their bands to participate actively in at least one small ensemble throughout every school year.

The small ensemble experience will (and should) vary with the individual student. For example, an outstanding high school clarinetist should be guided into more small ensemble work than merely the clarinet quartet. Perhaps a woodwind quartet or, better yet, a woodwind quintet can be organized. Another outlet would be performance, as clarinet soloist, with a string quartet. Small ensemble experience will undoubtedly aid in the development of musical growth and self-confidence. It should also help to meet individual differences regarding performance abilities of the students involved.

It is advisable to form groups of students who are similar in abilities and who are mutually compatible. Each group should

---

[2]Peters, p. 55–57.
[3]George Waln, "Start Your Ensembles in September," *The Instrumentalist*, September, 1962, p. 76.

have a student leader who would assume the responsibility of rehearsing the ensemble. This procedure would save valuable time for the instructor as well as provide opportunity for the student-in-charge to develop his leadership ability. The student leader of each group should be a fine musician and mature person who can command the respect and cooperation of his colleagues. Clearly, however, the teacher should arrange to work with each ensemble at least once a week.

Continuing the Ensemble Program. The problem of continuity has long plagued numerous small ensemble programs. In order for an ensemble program to be truly effective it *must* be continuous throughout the *entire* school year. A common mistake is to avoid starting the small ensembles until a month or two (or less!) before the annual spring contests or festivals. Effective ensemble playing demands a great deal of rehearsing and playing together over an extended period of time. Small ensembles should therefore be started soon after the opening of school in the fall in order to achieve the best results and derive the maximum benefits from this program.

Finding suitable materials for virtually any standard small ensemble should not be a problem. An abundance of fine literature is now available for groups at all levels of development. Small ensembles should, moreover, be encouraged to perform in public frequently. This provides genuine goals that the groups can work toward and is a fine aid in their development. Service clubs, civic organizations, parents' groups, and church societies provide excellent (and usually most appreciative) outlets for performances by chamber music groups.

The small ensemble program is of significant practical value to the total instrumental music program. Not only does it develop superior performers for the large instrumental groups, but it initiates an activity that can be a real source of satisfaction and pleasure throughout the students' entire life.

Selecting materials for wind and percussion ensembles

There is truly an abundance of fine musical literature for small ensembles. More is continually becoming available. The following is by no means a complete list since such a compilation would require well over an average size book in itself. Included here is a selective listing of representative works for most of the standard small ensemble combinations in the areas of woodwind, brass, and percussion. The grading is essentially arbitrary and intended only to give the reader a general classification concerning the technical and musical difficulty of the included compositions. The grading scale used includes the classifications of Easy, Moderately Easy, Moderately Difficult, and Difficult.

I. CLARINET

A. *Trios*

Cooke, "Suite for Three Clarinets" Oxford (Moderately Difficult)

Cox, "Divertissement" Henri Elkan (Moderately Difficult)

Moore, (arr.) "Twenty Trios" Willis (Easy to Moderately Easy)

Rosenthal, (arr.) "Eighteenth Century Trios" Marks (Moderately Easy)

Townsend, "Ballett Suite" Peters (Moderately Difficult)

Walker, "Trio in B Flat" Belwin (Moderately Easy)

Waterson, "First Grand Trio Concertante" Boosey & Hawkes (Difficult)

Voxman, (arr.) "Chamber Music, Volumes I and II" Rubank (Moderately Easy)

B. *Quartets* (four Bb clarinets unless otherwise indicated)

Bohm-Voxman, "Quartet in F" Rubank (Moderately Easy)

Desportes, "French Suite" (Difficult)

Gabrielski-Andraud, "Grand Quartet," No. 3, Opus 53 Southern (Difficult)

Karel, "Seascapes" Summy-Birchard (Moderately Difficult)

Mozart-Voxman, "Allegro" from *Quartet in C* (K. 157) (mixed quartet) Rubank (Moderately Difficult)

Sears, "Serenade in F" Pro Art (Moderately Easy)

Schumann-Simon, "Seven Miniatures" Boosey & Hawkes (Moderately Difficult)

Walker, "Aubade" (mixed quartet) Kendor (Moderately Easy)

Walker, "Quiet Brook" Kendor (Easy)

Wyman, "Les Joyeux Clarinets" (Mixed Quartet) MPHC (Moderately Difficult)

C. *Clarinet Choir*

Bach-Cailliet, "Awake, Awake, A Voice Is Calling" (Chorale) Leblanc (Easy)

Barnes, (arr.) "Robbins Collection of Classics for Balanced Clarinet Choir" Big 3 Music Corp. (Moderately Easy to Moderately Difficult)

Boellmann-Casteel, "Suite Gothique" Leblanc (Moderately Difficult)

Grieg-Feldsher, "Norwegian Dance #2" Aulos (Moderately Easy)

Handel-Webb, "Sarabande & Bouree" Kendor (Moderately Easy)

Humperdinck-DeJesu, "Hansel and Gretel" Hal Leonard (Easy)

Massenet-Cailliet, "Angelus" Leblanc (Moderately Easy)

Mendelssohn-Fote, "Variation Serieuses," Opus 54 Kendor (Difficult)

Mendelssohn-Webb, "Tarantella" Opus 102, No. 3 Kendor (Moderately Easy)

Moross, "Sonatina for Clarinet Choir" Chappell (Difficult)

Mozart-Cailliet, "Marriage of Figaro Overture" Leblanc (Difficult)

Mozart-Casteel & McCathren, "Overture to *Cosi Fan Tutte*" Kendor (Moderately Difficult)

Mozart-Frackenpohl, "Sinfonietta in B*b*" Shawnee Press (Moderately Difficult)

Mozart-Sacci, "Eine Kleine Nachtmusik Suite" Kendor (Moderately Difficult)

Schumann-Lang, "Träumerei" Charles Colin (Moderately Easy)

Voxman, (arr.) "Clarinet Choir Repertoire" Rubank (Moderately Easy to Moderately Difficult)

II. FLUTE—INCLUDING WOODWIND QUINTET

A. *Trios & Quartets*

Cohen, "Colonial Sketches" *Quartet* Belwin (Moderately Easy)

Gabrielski, "Grand Quartet in A Major" Edition Musicus (Difficult)

Gabrielski, "Grand Trio Concertante" Southern (Difficult)

Gurstenau, "First Quartet" Southern (Moderately Easy)

Hudadoff, "Twenty-Four Flute Trios" Pro Art (Moderately Easy)

McKay, "Sonatina Giocosa" *Quartet* Belwin (Moderately Difficult)

Neumann, "Grand Trio" Southern (Moderately Difficult)

Waln, "Classic Fantasy" *Trio* Kjos (Moderately Easy)

B. *Woodwind Quintet* (Flute, Clarinet, Oboe, Bassoon, and French Horn)

Andraud, (arr.) "Twenty-Two Quintets" Southern (Moderately Difficult to Difficult)

Arnold, "Three Shanties" Paterson (Moderately Difficult)

Barthe, "Passacaille" Rubank (Moderately Difficult)

Cohen, "Quintet No. 2" Belwin (Moderately Easy)

Danzi, "Quintet in E Minor," Associated Music Publishers (Moderately Difficult)

Etler, "Second Quintet" Associated Music Publishers (Difficult)

Hindemith, "Kleine Kammermusik" Associated Music Publishers (Difficult)

Lefebvre, "Suite," Opus 57 Belwin (Moderately Difficult)

Milhaud, "Chimney of King Rene" Southern (Difficult)

Ward, "Little Dance Suite" Mills (Moderately Easy)

III. ENSEMBLE COMBINATIONS WHICH INCLUDE THE OBOE

A. *Flute, Oboe, and Clarinet*

Andraud, (arr.) "18 Trios from Classic Masters" Southern (Moderately Difficult to Difficult)

Arnold, "Divertimento," Opus 37 Carl Fischer (Moderately Difficult)

DeWailly, "Aubade" Associated Music Publishers (Difficult)

Kriens, "Rondo des Lutins" Carl Fischer (Difficult)

Milhaud, "Sonate" Elkan-Vogel (Moderately Difficult)

Tustin, "Pastorale Modern" Barnhouse (Moderately Easy)

Walker, "Ballet Dance" Barnhouse (Moderately Easy)

B. *Oboe, Clarinet, and Bassoon*

Bozza, "Suite Breve in Trio" Southern (Difficult)

Gould, "Disciplines" Elkan-Vogel (Moderately Difficult)

Kesnar, "French Idyll" Cundy-Bettoney (Easy)

Martinu, "Four Madrigals" Associated Music Publishers (Difficult)

Milhaud, "Suite" Southern (Moderately Difficult)

Wissmer, "Serenade" Southern (Difficult)

IV. SAXOPHONE QUARTETS (Two altos, tenor, and baritone)

Bennett, "Saxophone Symphonette" Carl Fischer (Moderately Difficult)

Johnson, "Choral Fantasy" FitzSimons (Moderately Difficult)

Miller, "Quartet #2" Pro Art (Moderately Difficult)

Mozart-Thompson, "Marriage of Figaro Overture" Alfred (Difficult)

Schwarz, "Canzone" Rubank (Moderately Difficult)

Thompson, (arr.) "Londonderry Air" Alfred (Easy)

Walker, "Four Fancies" Belwin (Moderately Easy)

Weber-Thompson, "Overture to Der Freischutz" Alfred (Difficult)

Yoder, (arr.) "Jericho" Kjos (Moderately Difficult)

V. ENSEMBLE COMBINATIONS WHICH INCLUDE THE BASSOON

A. *Flute, Clarinet, and Bassoon*

Kummer, "Trio in F" Rubank (Moderately Difficult)

Piket, "Trio" Omega (Moderately Difficult)

Piston, "Three Pieces" Southern (Difficult)

Zoeller, "Three Virtuos" Southern (Difficult)

B. *Two Clarinets and Bassoon*

McKay, "Blue Tapestry" Barnhouse (Moderately Difficult)

Mozart, "Five Divertimenti, K. 229" Associated Music Publishers (Moderately Difficult)

C. *Woodwind Quartet* (Flute, Oboe, Clarinet, and Bassoon)

Bridge, "Divertimenti" Boosey & Hawkes (Difficult)

Filippi, "In Nostalgic Mood" Elkan-Vogel (Easy)

Goepfart-Andraud, "Quartet for Woodwinds" Southern (Difficult)

Grieg, "Three Little Pieces" Carl Fischer (Moderately Easy)

Mozart-Richter, "Adagio" Music Publishers' Holding Corp. (Moderately Difficult)

Schumann, "Scenes from Childhood" Witmark (Moderately Easy)

Tustin, "Improvisation #1" Barnhouse (Moderately Difficult)

VI. TRUMPET TRIOS

Clarke, "Three Aces" Fillmore (Difficult)

Knight, (arr.) "Ten Trios for Trumpeters" Mills (Easy to Moderately Easy)

McKay, "Three Cadets" Barnhouse (Moderately Difficult)

Mendelssohn-Smith, "Rondo Capriccioso" Mills (Difficult)

Muczynski, "Trumpet Trio, Opus 11" G. Schirmer (Moderately Difficult)

Ostling, (arr.) "Album of Trumpet Trios" Belwin (Easy to Moderately Easy)

Stein, "Trio for Trumpets" Presser (Difficult)

Vandercook, "Aces of the Air" Rubank (Moderately Easy)

Williams, "Orion" Chas. Colin (Moderately Difficult)

VII. TRUMPET QUARTETS

Artot, "Twelve Quartets" Cundy-Bettoney (Moderately Easy to Moderately Difficult)

Bach-Johnson, "Five Bach Chorales" Rubank (Moderately Easy)

Ellmenreich-Irons, "Spinning Song" Rubank (Moderately Easy)

Gillis, "Second Sonatina" Boosey & Hawkes (Difficult)

Johnson, "In the Forest" Belwin (Easy)

Leidzen, "The Four Heralds" Bourne (Moderately Difficult)

Ostransky, "Dance Suite" Rubank (Moderately Difficult)

Simpson, "Sonatine" Carl Fischer (Easy)

VIII. BRASS QUARTET (Two Trumpets and Two Trombones or Baritones)

Bergsma, "Suite" Carl Fischer (Difficult)

Johnson, "Caprice in G Minor" Rubank (Moderately Easy)

Lawton, (arr.) "Quartets for Brass" (in Two Volumes) Oxford (Easy to Moderately Easy)

McKay, "Interlude for Brass Quartet" Barnhouse (Easy)

Morris, (arr.) "Second Album for Brass Quartet" Ludwig (Easy to Moderately Easy)

Whear, "Prelude and Rondo" Barnhouse (Moderately Easy)

Whitney, "Brass Quartet #1" Carl Fischer (Moderately Difficult)

IX. BRASS QUARTET (Two Trumpets, French Horn, Trombone or Baritone)

Bach-Johnson, "Bach Chorales for Brass Quartet" Rubank (Moderately Easy)

Bach-King, "March, Chorale, and Fugue" Robert King (Moderately Difficult)

Barnes, (arr.) "Album for Brass Quartet" (Volume #1) (Easy to Moderately Easy)

Hering, (arr.) "Early Classics" Carl Fischer (Easy)

Hovhaness, "Sharagen and Fugue" Robert King (Difficult)

Lovelock, "Three Pieces for Brass Quartet" Chappell (Moderately Easy)

Parshall, "Quartet in B*b*" Belwin (Moderately Difficult)

Schmutz, "Air and Scherzo" Carl Fischer (Moderately Difficult)

X. BRASS QUINTET (Two Trumpets, French Horn, Trombone (Baritone) and Tuba)

Arnold, "Quintet for Brass" Carl Fischer (Difficult)

Bach-Beeler, "If Thou Be Near" Rubank (Moderately Easy)

Bach-Gordon, "Five Pieces for Brass Quintet" Witmark (Moderately Easy)

Dieterich, "Horizons" Rubank (Easy)

Pezel-Menken, "Sonata #5" Boosey & Hawkes (Moderately Difficult)

Schmutz, "Prelude & Gavotte" FitzSimons (Moderately Difficult)

Simon, "First Quintet for Brass" Music Publishers Holding Corporation (Moderately Difficult)

XI. BRASS SEXTET (Two Trumpets, French Horn, Trombone, Baritone, and Tuba)

Bach-Johnson, "Four Chorales for Brass Sextet" Rubank (Moderately Easy)

Busch, "Prelude and Choral" (with Tympani) Carl Fischer (Moderately Difficult)

McKay, "Prelude and Allegro" Barnhouse (Moderately Difficult)

Simon-Voxman, "Four Pieces for Brass Sextet" Rubank (Moderately Easy)

XII. BRASS CHOIR

Anderson, "Suite of Carols" Mills (Moderately Difficult)

Barnes, (arr.) "Robbins Collection for Brass Choir" Big Three (Moderately Easy to Moderately Difficult)

Findlay, (arr.) "Junior Brass Choir" Carl Fischer (Easy to Moderately Easy)

King, "Prelude and Fugue for Brass Choir" Robert King (Moderately Difficult)

Tyra, "Suite for Brass Choir and Tympani" Southern (Difficult)

Uber, "Gettysburg" Edition Musicus (Difficult)

XIII. FRENCH HORN QUARTETS

Artot, (arr.) "Twelve Quartets" Cundy-Bettoney (Moderately Difficult to Difficult)

Hindemith, "Concerto for Four Horns" Robert King (Difficult)

Howe, (arr.) "Two Dozen Horn Quartets" Morris (Easy to Moderately Easy)

Koepke, "Introduction and Scherzo" Rubank (Moderately Difficult)

Lesur, "Five Interludes" International (Difficult)

McKay, "American Panorama" Carl Fischer (Moderately Difficult)

McKay, "Petite Suite, Opus 15" Carl Fischer (Moderately Difficult)

Mayer, "Four Little Pieces" Southern (Moderately Easy)

Ostransky, "Aeolian Suite" Rubank (Moderately Easy)

Ostransky, "Velvet and Tweed" Rubank (Moderately Difficult)

Pottag, (arr.) "Quartet Album for French Horns" Belwin (Moderately Easy)

XIV. TROMBONE TRIOS (with piano)

Barnes, "Three Debonaires" Ludwig (Moderately Difficult)

Johnson, "The Cavaliers" Rubank (Easy)

Mozart-Ostrander, "Suite for Three Trombones" Edition Musicus (Moderately Difficult)

Ostransky, "Contest Trio #1" Rubank (Moderately Difficult)

Schaefer, "Fancy Free" Fillmore (Difficult)

XV. TROMBONE QUARTETS

Bassett, "Quartet for Trombones" Robert King (Moderately Difficult)

DeBueris, "Trombone Fantasie" Southern (Difficult)

Koepke, "Scherzo Caprice" Rubank (Moderately Easy)

McKay, "Festival March" Barnhouse (Moderately Difficult)

Muller, (arr.) "Twenty Trombone Quartets" Cundy-Bettoney (Moderately Easy to Moderately Difficult)

XVI. PERCUSSION

Blount, "Modulation" (Three Snare Drums, Cymbals, and Bass Drum) Fillmore (Difficult)

Blount, "The Conquerors" (Snare Drum Trio) Fillmore (Difficult)

Buggert, "Drummer's Canzonetta" (Snare Drum Trio) Rubank (Difficult)

Christian, "Allemande" (Bells and Xylophone) Creative (Moderately Easy)

Firth, "Encore in Jazz" (Timpani, Three Drums, Vibraphone and Indian Drum, Marimba & Cow Bell, Bongos, Conga Drum, Dance Drums) Carl Fischer (Difficult)

Firth, "Roll-Off Rhumba" (Timpani, Snare Drum, Military Drum, Bongos, Conga Drum, Cymbals and Bass Drum) Carl Fischer (Moderately Difficult)

Firth, "Six Little Indians" (Timpani, Tambourine, Snare Drum, Field Drum & Wood Block, Crash Cymbal and suspended cymbal, Bass Drum and Small Gong) Carl Fischer (Easy)

Flagello, "Divertimento" (Piano, Bells, Chimes, Vibraharp, and Xylophone) Music for Percussion (Difficult)

Hankins, "Five Up Front" (Three Snare Drums, Cymbals, and Bass Drum) Fillmore (Moderately Difficult)

Hankins, "Snares Forward" (Snare Drum Trio) Fillmore (Easy)

Harr, "The Downfall of Paris" (Three Snare Drums, Cymbals, Bass Drum, Bell Lyre, and Piano) Carl Fischer (Moderately Difficult)

Harr, "Ticonderoga" (Two Snare Drums and Bass Drum) Rubank (Moderately Difficult)

Harr, "Valley Forge" (Three Snare Drums and Bass Drum) Rubank (Moderately Difficult)

Heney, "Air Express" (Two Snare Drums, Cymbals, and Bass Drum) Fillmore (Difficult)

Hovhaness, "Burning House Overture" (Bells and Marimba) Peters (Moderately Difficult)

Schinstine, "Accent on Rhythm" (Snare Drum Quartet) Southern (Moderately Difficult)

Shirley and Buggert, "Rudimental Roulade" (Three Snare Drums, Bass Drum, and Cymbals) Rubank (Moderately Difficult)

Smith, "Suite for Drums" (Three Snare Drums) Carl Fischer (Moderately Difficult)

CHAPTER 5

How to Achieve In-Service Professional Growth

In a recent article a group of leading American educators expressed the feeling that "quality of teachers is the most critical problem area in education today."[1] The American public in general is becoming increasingly cognizant of the need for quality teachers and quality teaching on all educational levels. A number of widely read journals, periodicals, and newspapers are now (and have been for some time) publishing articles dealing with this problem. Largely as a result of trying to solve this dilemma, teachers' salaries and working conditions have improved significantly during the last decade. As Fischer points out: "The change is not, however, without its unpleasant side, for while the glare of the spotlight may lend the teacher something of a halo, it also reveals his flaws with a minimum of mercy."[2] It is the purpose of this chapter to explore this problem and to discuss some of its ramifications.

---

[1] Jules Harcourt, "A Study of the Membership of PHI DELTA KAPPA," *Phi Delta Kappan*, June, 1965, p. 515.
[2] John H. Fischer, "Why Teach?" *NEA Journal*, April, 1962, p. 31.

What makes a "quality teacher"?

Perhaps somewhere short of being "all things to all students" is the "ideal" teacher. It is undoubtedly true that the term "quality teacher" means many things to many people. Moreover, it should be recognized that it is entirely possible for any given teacher to be regarded as "excellent" and "poor" by equally capable students, and indeed by parents and school officials as well. As one professor candidly states: "I've had some students who have asked me to help them shape their entire professional futures and others who hated my guts. A's good teacher may be B's schnook."[3] The purpose here is to attempt to define the basic qualities and characteristics which, when combined, tend to make up a teacher who would generally be held in high esteem by most thinking people, both in and out of the education profession.

The Teacher's Personality. The teacher's role within the context of the school setting is a great deal more important than many realize. Karl Menninger states: "I have often said that teachers and policemen ought to be the highest paid and most carefully selected officials in the community, because they have the most important responsibilities."[4] The psychiatrist Joost Meerloo suggests that: "Teachers are models second in importance only to parents and sometimes even more important than parents."[5]

Of crucial importance, therefore, is the teacher's personality. Such questions as the following need to be raised: Does the teacher possess emotional stability and self-control, remaining calm and using restraint under stress and strain? Does he have a balanced sense of humor and do students respond in a positive way to his friendly, cheerful, and understanding nature? Does the teacher possess and reflect the quality of *empathy*? Meerloo points out: "The neurotic teacher who brings in his own unsolved, childish patterns can do the child a lot of harm regardless of the teacher's technical training."[6]

---

[3]Donald C. Emerson, quoted in: "Sponsored Research—Its Effect on Teachers" *College Management*, December, 1966, p. 21.

[4]Karl Menninger, *Love Against Hate* (New York: Harcourt, Brace, and Company, 1942), p. 257.

[5]Joost Meerloo, "Guidance in an Age of Technology," *Teachers College Record*, May, 1961, p. 594.

[6]*Ibid.*, p. 591.

The importance of subject matter should never be underestimated since every teacher needs a thorough knowledge and command of the subject(s) he teaches. Moreover, he needs to keep this knowledge up to date. It is difficult at best for students to learn from a teacher who does not have a deep understanding of his subject matter as well as the ability to organize and present it in an interesting, stimulating, and meaningful manner.

The Inspired Teacher. In order to inspire others it is imperative that the teacher himself be inspired and enthusiastic about teaching in general and his subject in particular. Near the end of his long career as a master teacher Professor William Lyon Phelps of Yale declared:

> In my mind, teaching is not merely a life work, a profession, an occupation, a struggle; it is a passion. I love to teach. I love to teach as a painter loves to paint, as a musician loves to play, as a singer loves to sing, as a strong man rejoices to run a race. Teaching is an art—an art so great and so difficult to master that a man or woman can spend a long life at it without realizing much more than his limitations and mistakes and his distance from the ideal.[7]

In addition, the superior teacher must possess the ability to arouse discussion and to tolerate differences of opinion. He must be able to evaluate fairly and stimulate his students to critical thought. A good deal more could be said about the make-up of a quality teacher. Clearly, only general characteristics have been presented. Pragmatically, one must conclude that all schools will probably never be staffed entirely by teachers of this caliber. On the other hand, America is at a point in its history when poor and mediocre teaching must be reduced to an absolute minimum.

Using mechanical rating devices and staffing schools with excellent teachers

Selective merit pay is a proposition open to question. The numerous innocuous merit rating systems found in the majority of school systems are noncontroversial. William Carleton cogently states:

---

[7]William Lyon Phelps, quoted in: *A Study Guide to Evaluation* (mimeographed). Scotch Plains-Fanwood (New Jersey) Public Schools, 1961, p. 2.

All mechanical methods of rating teaching and scholarship are inhibitive and oppressive. They tend to exalt form over substance and spirit, and they stack the cards in favor of the mediocre and against the gifted. The process of determining who is a good teacher is a slow, gradual, informal, and spontaneous one. The true verdict comes out of a general consensus, developed over the years by students, colleagues, and administrators on the spot.[8]

Teaching is (and probably always will be) more of an *art* than a *science*. Therefore, a totally honest, fair, and impartial merit pay system is very nearly an impossibility. As Irving Katz suggests: "The net effect of merit pay is discontent, friction, and discord within a school staff."[9]

This, of course, does not obviate the urgency for staffing schools with excellent teachers as soon as possible. It would, however, be extremely naive to think that there is a quick and easy solution to this complex problem. Better working conditions and increased salaries are helping to attract more capable people to the profession. But the problem goes far deeper than this. There would seem to be a definite need for much more *careful screening* of prospective teachers by teacher-training institutions. No profession as yet has been able to eliminate *all* undesirable candidates, but it seems that more could and should be done along these lines within the education profession. Those who are found to be psychologically, emotionally, or intellectually unfit for careers as teachers should be eliminated *before* they are allowed to enter the profession. This should be done as early as possible in the student's college career.

Selecting Staff Personnel. A crucial point of screening is that it should be done by officials of the various school systems. It has been wisely said that one of the most important duties of the superintendent of schools is the selection of staff personnel. This responsibility should not be delegated to inexperienced and unqualified people. If possible, it is salutary to have the candidate

---

[8]William G. Carleton, "Letter to a new Ph.D," *Teachers College Record*, December, 1961, p. 201.

[9]Irving Katz, "Why I Oppose Selective Merit Pay," *Phi Delta Kappan*, January, 1961, p. 161.

appear before a committee comprised of both administrators and teachers in the candidate's subject area.

Finally, tenure should be granted only to those who clearly demonstrate superior teaching ability. This should be a collective decision based on the most objective evaluations possible by a number of people in the areas of both administration and instruction. In reaching this decision it should be remembered that a teacher's retention or dismissal should be based on his competence and effectiveness *as a teacher* and not on personal bias either for or against the teacher. As Glen Law points out:

> Surprisingly, a great many dismissals in all phases of employment in vocations and in professions are not the result of incompetence. Dismissal is more frequently the result of faulty personal adjustment or irritating relations. It can even result from over-competence. Retention, in any case, cannot be solely justified on a person's alacrity to stay out of the boss' way and not irritate him.[10]

Tenure should never be granted in a quasi-automatic fashion as is frequently the case.

On-the-Job Supervision. The weak or routine teacher can be greatly helped by effective and stimulating supervision on the job. The principal and area supervisor can play key roles here by attempting to bring out the best personal and professional qualities of their teachers. It is they who should take the lead in setting the educational tone for the school. Indeed, their influence, for better or for worse, is usually pervasive within the school setting. Inadequate administrative and supervisory personnel have no place in the schools of today. Even excellent teachers usually find it difficult to function under inept educational leadership. Finally, a teacher who is proven to be incompetent should not be allowed to continue in the profession. No tenure law should prevent his dismissal.

There can be little doubt of the urgent need for quality teaching on all educational levels. As the education profession matures it must become increasingly aware of its responsibilities to the

---

[10]Glen C. Law, *The Urgency of New Leadership in Higher Education* (Stamford: Press-Tige Publishing Co., 1962), p. 56.

people it serves. With education's growth into a mature and honored profession must come the ability to be highly selective of the candidates who seek to enter it and equally demanding of the professionals who continue to actively serve it.

What makes the school instrumental music teacher effective?

What are the ingredients that combine to make an effective and successful instrumental music teacher in today's schools? One who is an excellent musician and little else will probably fall considerably short of modern job requirements. One does not have to look very far to find splendid musicians with an abundance of technical knowledge who are failing on the job.

In order to better understand the responsibilities of an instrumental music teacher one should perhaps consider his many roles. Few will debate the point that first and foremost he must be a fine musician and capable teacher. Yet he must be much more. W. Clyde Duvall indicates that "he is a combination of five people: musician, teacher, youth worker, administrator, and showman. And he knows that each one of his roles is important."[11]

Daniel Henkin states: "In addition to the musical aspects, there is the multi-faced 'business side' of being a band director—down-to-earth, basic, and essential."[12] He further indicates the director's responsibility as a public relations man, a production manager, and organizer, an adviser, a repair man, and a finance man "in addition to being primarily an educator and musician!"[13] One can readily concur with Mursell's comment that "the average working music educator is far busier than he has any business to be."[14] As Yoder suggests:

> There never was a lazy band director, at least I have never seen one. In our profession there is so much to do in such a comparatively short amount of time that only those with "drive" can make the grade.[15]

---

[11]W. Clyde Duvall, *The High School Band Director's Handbook* (Englewood Cliffs: Prentice-Hall, Inc., 1960), p. 2.

[12]Daniel J. Henkin, "Just a Band Director," *The Instrumentalist*, November, 1962, p. 40.

[13]Henkin, p. 40.

[14]James L. Mursell, *Music Education*, p. 6.

[15]Paul Yoder, "Personal Dynamics," *The Instrumentalist*, August, 1961, p. 48.

Professional growth versus stagnation

What then can the instrumental teacher do to improve himself in his multi-roled profession? Perhaps the most important area is that of professional growth. In order to keep abreast of the latest happenings and new ideas in his field, the instrumental teacher should avail himself of the opportunity to attend clinics or professional meetings (both in music specifically and education generally), read professional literature, commence or continue graduate study, and attend other schools' instrumental music concerts. Tape recordings and/or movies of one's teaching and conducting will provide many insights into ways of improving one's professional competence.

It is also of considerable importance to continue development on one's major medium of musical expression. Too many instrumental music teachers appear to be lacking in this significant area. Many directors tend to neglect their professional growth. Yet it is surely true that fine instrumental organizations are developed by teachers who continue to grow educationally and musically as they pursue their professions.

Typical pitfalls to avoid

Frequently an instrumental music teacher will spend so much time in the development of his groups that he will fail to see the *total educational picture* of the school in which he occupies a professional position. Indeed, some teachers seem to be so involved with their own areas of responsibility that they know little or nothing of the choral, general, or elementary music programs. These are serious pitfalls. When the instrumental teacher becomes this busy (whether actual or imaginary) he should seek to alter his overall perspective and reconsider his role within the context of his total educational setting.

Another serious pitfall (both musically and educationally) is that of becoming so occupied with performing groups and public performances that music per se tends to assume a rather incidental role. It would seem of great importance to include such subjects as music theory and harmony, music history, and music literature in the instrumental music program. Much can be done in these areas during the instrumental rehearsal. If possible, the director should offer advanced instruction in these subjects to students who are obviously interested and gifted musically.

Finding effective human relations and beneficial outside interests

It goes without saying that the instrumental music teacher must be skilled in the area of human relations. It is imperative that he relate to his administrators, fellow faculty members, students, and students' parents in a positive way. Few other school personnel are in the public eye as frequently and consistently as the instrumental teacher. He is, in many ways, a super-salesman selling an excellent product—music. Yet, he will find selling his product much easier if he sells himself first.

It is also essential for the instrumental teacher to cultivate a wide range of interests and hobbies outside of his field. The wise instrumental teacher will develop a schedule that will permit time for such activities. This should benefit all concerned since a tired, bedraggled, and cross teacher is usually not able to function effectively on the job.

Evaluating teacher effectiveness and instruction

The two instruments of evaluation that follow are intended to provide the teacher with checklists or guidelines to facilitate professional growth in his area of competence. Clearly, it is not the intent here to suggest that these are perfect instruments for measuring teacher effectiveness and evaluating teacher competence. Rather, if they will cause the teacher to look at himself in an objective way for the purpose of trying to improve his professional competence, they will have served their purpose.

If the "Checklist for Student Reaction to Instructor and Instruction" is used, its stated purpose ("to obtain information which may lead to the improvement of instruction") should be made quite clear to the students. In addition, it would be well for the teacher to discuss the entire scale with his students *before* they proceed to complete it. Many valuable insights can accrue from this device if it is properly used and the results kept in their proper perspective.

A STATEMENT OF TEACHER EFFECTIVENESS[16]

Scotch Plains-Fanwood Public Schools

Scotch Plains, N.J.

Name	Needs To Grow	Shows Continued Growth	Demonstrates Effectiveness
I. *Personal Attributes*			
A. Impression, Speech, Bearing			
B. Character and Personality			
C. Enthusiasm			
D. Human Relations			
II. *Professional Attainments*			
A. Command of subject matter			
B. Understanding the nature of learning			
C. Scope of interest— wider horizons			
D. Alertness to needs, present and future			
E. Professionality and growth			
III. *Instructional Leadership*			
A. The environment for learning—classroom atmosphere			
B. Classroom organization & control			
C. Preparation & planning —goals			
D. Teaching techniques			

[16]From *Guidelines Toward the Improvement of Instruction*, Scotch Plains-Fanwood Public Schools, Scotch Plains, New Jersey. Used by permission.

E. Articulation in subject matter _____			
F. Motivation, stimulation, creativity _____			
G. Identification of and provision for individual differences & potential _____			
H. Evaluation _____			
I. Pupil growth _____			

IV. *Plans of action for further growth*:

_____

_____

_____

_____

_____

_____

_____

_____

_____

_____

_____

_____

_____

V. *Comments*:_____

_____

_____

_____

_____

VI. *Conclusions*:

☐   A teacher who is clearly effective and efficient who has our unqualified confidence in his continuing professional contribution.

☐ A teacher who demonstrates increasing effectiveness and exhibits both willingness and promise for continuing growth.

☐ A teacher who is not now meeting our expectations for effectiveness and who must show considerable growth in order to make a successful contribution to our school system. Recommendation for reemployment or salary increment is in doubt.

☐ A teacher who shows little promise at this time of making a successful contribution to our educational program. Not recommended for further employment here.

_____   _____
       TEACHER   DATE

_____
       EVALUATOR

CHECKLIST FOR STUDENT REACTION TO INSTRUCTOR AND INSTRUCTION[17]

Instructions: *Do not sign your name or put any mark of identification on paper.*

The following is a list of qualities that, taken together, tend to make any instructor the kind of instructor he is. It is admitted that no instructor is "ideal" in all of these qualities but some approach this ideal to a greater extent than do others. *In order to obtain information which may lead to the improvement of instruction,* you are asked to evaluate your instructor and the instruction he provides on the indicated qualities by marking an X in the box on the line which most nearly describes your instructor or his instruction with reference to the quality you are considering:

PERSONAL APPRAISAL

I. KNOWLEDGE OF SUBJECT

With regard to knowledge of the subject, I would say the instructor:

_____

[17]Adapted from *Northeast Missouri State College Scale for Student Evaluation of Instruction,* Northeast Missouri State College, Kirksville. Used by Permission.

( ) 1. Knows it thoroughly
( ) 2. Knows it fairly well
( ) 3. Does not know it very well
( ) 4. Knows it poorly

II. PRESENTATION OF SUBJECT

In relation to my other courses, I would say this course was:

( ) 1. Unusually well presented
( ) 2. Well presented
( ) 3. About average
( ) 4. Poorly presented
( ) 5. Very poorly presented

III. STUDENT-TEACHER RELATIONSHIP

During the class period I believe that:

( ) 1. A cordial and cooperative feeling prevails
( ) 2. Neither good will nor antagonism prevails
( ) 3. The teacher tends to antagonize the student

IV. EXPLANATIONS

( ) 1. Unusually clear
( ) 2. Fairly clear
( ) 3. Not very clear
( ) 4. Definitely confusing

V. ANSWERING QUESTIONS

When questions are asked in class I believe the teacher:

( ) 1. Answers them fully and directly
( ) 2. Answers them partially
( ) 3. Evades the question
( ) 4. Does not answer them

VI. INTEREST IN STUDENTS

When dealing with students I believe the teacher is:

( ) 1. Always considerate and courteous
( ) 2. Usually considerate and courteous
( ) 3. Sometimes inconsiderate and discourteous
( ) 4. Always inconsiderate and discourteous

VII. SELF-CONFIDENCE

I believe the teacher is:

( ) 1. Usually sure of himself
( ) 2. Fairly self-confident
( ) 3. Usually uncertain of himself

VIII. SENSE OF HUMOR

I believe the teacher:

( ) 1. Has a keen and pleasing sense of humor
( ) 2. Rather sober and serious, somewhat humorous at times
( ) 3. Is far too serious

IX. PERSONAL APPEARANCE

With regard to appearance I would say the teacher is:

( ) 1. Always well groomed
( ) 2. Fairly well groomed but sometimes negligent in keeping clothes neat and clean
( ) 3. Usually careless and untidy in dress

X. PERSONAL PECULIARITIES

In my opinion the teacher is:

( ) 1. Entirely free from annoying and distracting mannerisms
( ) 2. Moderately free from annoying and distracting mannerisms
( ) 3. Consistently exhibiting annoying and distracting mannerisms (List on back of paper if you desire.)

XI. PUNCTUALITY

In the area of punctuality I would say that the teacher:

( ) 1. Is very punctual in meeting classes
( ) 2. Is fairly punctual in meeting classes
( ) 3. Is often lacking in punctuality

XII. VOICE

With regard to voice quality I would say the teacher:

( ) 1. Has a clear and pleasing voice
( ) 2. Speaks fairly well
( ) 3. Has poor voice quality, words not clear, weak expression

ASSIGNMENTS AND EXAMINATIONS

I. ASSIGNMENTS

When making assignments I would say that the teacher is:

( ) 1. Always definite
( ) 2. Usually definite
( ) 3. Indefinite
( ) 4. Very indefinite

II. FREQUENCY OF EXAMINATIONS

I think that examinations in this class were given:

( ) 1. Too often
( ) 2. About often enough
( ) 3. Too seldom

III. EXAMINATION QUESTIONS

I think that the questions on the examinations were:

( ) 1. Always clearly stated
( ) 2. Usually well stated
( ) 3. Confusing as to meaning

IV. ADMINISTRATION OF EXAMINATIONS

When taking examinations I think that students were:

( ) 1. Always well supervised
( ) 2. Usually well supervised
( ) 3. Poorly supervised

V. FAIRNESS IN GRADING

With regard to grading, I think the teacher:

( ) 1. Is very fair and impartial
( ) 2. Occasionally shows favoritism
( ) 3. Consistently shows favoritism

COURSE APPRAISAL

I. COURSE

In relation to my other courses, I would say that this course was:

( ) 1. Very difficult
( ) 2. Difficult

( ) 3. Average
( ) 4. Easy
( ) 5. Very easy

II. HOME WORK

When considered in relation to my other courses, I would say that this course required:

( ) 1. More preparation
( ) 2. About the same preparation
( ) 3. Less preparation

III. OUTSIDE PRACTICE

I would say that the outside practice assigned for this course was:

( ) 1. Closely integrated with the class work
( ) 2. Not closely related
( ) 3. Merely busy-work

IV. VALUE OF COURSE

I feel that this course will prove to be:

( ) 1. Very valuable
( ) 2. Valuable
( ) 3. Of little value
( ) 4. A waste of time

V. ENJOYMENT

In relation to my other courses, I would say that this course was:

( ) 1. Very enjoyable
( ) 2. Enjoyable
( ) 3. Average
( ) 4. Dull
( ) 5. Very dull

TEACHER RANK

With relation to other teachers I have had, I would rank this teacher in the:

( ) 1. Top ten percent

(   ) 2. Top twenty-five percent
(   ) 3. Top fifty percent
(   ) 4. Lower fifty percent
(   ) 5. Lower twenty-five percent
(   ) 6. Lower ten percent

DO NOT SIGN YOUR NAME

II

TEACHING THE WOODWINDS FOR INDIVIDUAL SKILLS

CHAPTER 6

The Clarinet

The clarinet is generally considered to be the basic woodwind instrument, and it is probably true that there are more clarinet students in our schools than all of the other woodwinds combined. Moreover, the clarinet family, when fully represented, forms the basis of the modern concert band. The purpose of this chapter is to discuss a number of important aspects of clarinet performance and pedagogy as well as developing specific individual skills within the framework of selected clarinet solo literature. The bibliography is presented for those who wish to pursue specific problems deeply.

Selecting instructional materials

There is an abundance of instructional literature for the clarinet. The following materials constitute a representative listing which ranges from beginning methods to étude books for the advanced clarinetist.

Beginning Methods

Universal Fundamental Method .... Universal
Belwin Clarinet Method, Book I .... Belwin
Rubank Elementary Method .... Rubank

Intermediate Methods

Rubank Intermediate Method .... Rubank
Belwin Clarinet Method, Book II .... Belwin
Universal Follow-Up Method .... Universal

Medium Advanced Methods

416 Progressive Daily Studies   F. Kroepsch,
(Book I) .... Carl Fischer
Bäermann Method for Clarinet .... Carl Fischer
(Second Division, Revised by Langenus)
Rose 32 Etudes .... Carl Fischer
Eleven Modern Etudes .... Druart-Leblanc

Advanced Methods

18 Etudes for the Clarinet .... Jean-Jean, Alfred
416 Progressive Daily Studies   F. Kroepsch,
(Books II and IV) .... Carl Fischer
Classical Studies .... Voxman-Rubank
(Based on works of Bach and Handel)
24 Studies in All Keys .... Stark-Cundy-Bettoney
Thirty Caprices .... Cavallini-Carl Fischer
20 Grande Etudes .... Rode-Rose, M. Baron Co.
16 Etudes Modernes pour Clarinette .... Jean-Jean, Buffet-
                                                                    Crampon & Cie
The Twentieth Century Clarinetist .... Sigel-Franco Colombo

**Choosing a clarinet, clarinet recordings, and care of
the clarinet**

The teacher will diminish the problems of clarinet teaching by
a careful selection of the instrument. Obviously a first-line instrument should be purchased if possible. Consideration should be
given to the overall pitch level of the instrument in relation to the
pitch level of his organizations. A recent study has revealed that
many professional symphony clarinetists would like to be able
to play up to a pitch of 441 or 442.[1] It is most essential that the
clarinet be in tune with itself. If the instructor is not a woodwind
specialist, it is recommended that he engage the help of a person
who is when making the final selection of an instrument. Virtually

---

[1] Austin McDowell, "Are We Teaching the Clarinet Properly?" *The Instrumentalist,* December, 1966, p. 74.

all clarinet manufacturing firms provide detailed instructions with regard to the care of the instrument. Clarinets that are well made and mechanically sound can be played extensively for years with only minor repairs. A complete overhaul of the clarinet is recommended by most authorities every one or two years, depending on the quality of the instrument and the care it receives.

The following recordings demonstrate the clarinet and clarinet family:

> "The Instruments of the Orchestra" (with narrator and performed by first desk men of the Vienna State Opera Orchestra), Vanguard, records #VRS-1017 and VRS-1018.
>
> "Contest Solos for the Clarinet Family"—10 solos for Eb, Bb, Alto, Bass, and Contrabass Clarinet. Donald McCathren, Clarinetist. Distributed by Selmer.
>
> "Clarinet Contest Music"—Donald McGinnis, Clarinetist. Selmer record No. 2944.
>
> "Music for Clarinet Choir"—State University College at Fredonia, New York Clarinet Choir. Available from Kendor, Inc., Delevan, New York.
>
> "Clarinet Music for Contest"—David Hite, Clarinetist. Available from Southern Music Co., San Antonio, Texas.
>
> "Concertino for Clarinet and Orchestra" by Weber. Anthony Gigliotti, Clarinetist, and the Philadelphia Orchestra. Columbia #ML 4629.
>
> "Contest Music for the Clarinet"—Richard Weerts, Clarinetist, Austin Custom Records, Austin, Texas.

Developing tone production on the clarinet

The area of tone production on the clarinet is not only important but vital to fine musical performance. The problem appears to be a pervasive one that plagues many instrumental directors in our schools. In its very genesis the production of a rich, flexible, and idiomatic tone on the clarinet must originate in the mind of the clarinetist. In other words, the player must have a concept of the sound he would like to produce. This concept is usually never a static one. Even the most advanced players frequently seek to alter slightly some aspect of their tone qualities. A concept of a fine clarinet tone can be developed and nurtured in a number of ways. Surely one of the best is to listen to an excellent clarinetist perform in person. The neophyte clarinetist would do well to avail himself of the opportunity to hear as many fine "live" clarinet performances as possible. Listening to fine clarinet recordings is another way to develop a concept of tone. One also frequently hears some excellent clarinet work on movie sound tracks as well as on the radio and television. A good concept of tone seems to be the *sine qua non* of producing a fine tone on the clarinet.

It is probably incorrect to label any certain type of tone quality as the "ideal" or the only desirable tone for which to strive. Clarinet tone quality is, on its higher levels of development, a highly controversial issue and very subjective in nature. Actually, it is undoubtedly true that every professional clarinetist and advanced student of the clarinet has his own distinctive tone quality. A high degree of pitch sensitivity is also essential for producing a fine clarinet sound. Tone quality and playing in tune within one's own instrument, as well as with other instruments, are also very much interrelated. The practice of listening carefully to one's own tone should be cultivated.

Correct Clarinet Embouchure. A good embouchure is obviously of great importance as it relates to (and is interrelated with) tone production. In general, a good embouchure might be described as one which allows the clarinetist both to produce an idiomatic sound and to sing on his instrument. It should make playing from pianissimo to fortissimo an easy matter. This embouchure would not distort the tone on the forte level and would permit fluidity on the mezzo forte and piano levels. Finally, it would make the achievement of intensity of tone quality in the climax of phrases possible. This is indeed a large order for any clarinetist to fill and the achievement of these qualities marks the truly superior player.

The position of the mouthpiece in the mouth has much to do with tone quality. The player's lower lip should be stretched securely against the lower teeth and the mouthpiece laid over the lower lip. The mouth should then close naturally around the mouthpiece. Approximately one-half of the red of the lower lip should be rolled over the lower teeth. The player's upper teeth should lie on the mouthpiece approximately one-half inch from the tip, whereas the lower lip should press the reed at approximately three-quarters of an inch from its tip. The cheeks should not be blown out nor the lower jaw dropped. (See Figure 6-A.)

Figure 6–A   Clarinet Embouchure

Closely related to achieving a fine tone are the mouthpiece and reed. It is at this point that so many inexperienced clarinet players waste time, money, and effort. In short, some players are forever looking for the ideal mouthpiece and the ideal reed. They are endlessly trying out mouthpiece after mouthpiece and every brand of reed available in the hope of finding the perfect combination. It is probably better to find a good mouthpiece and learn to adjust to it. Equally important is the need to find a good reed. The aspiring clarinetist should also learn to adjust reeds as soon as possible. Two other factors that might be taken for granted, but are none the less intertwined in producing a fine clarinet tone, are the necessity of an erect (but not rigid) posture and a first-line instrument.

An open, relaxed throat is essential to a fine tone. Conversely a tense, constricted throat will have a deleterious effect on tone quality. The tone should never be forced through the clarinet. Many clarinetists have the fallacious idea that to get a good tone one must use a hard reed and blow with considerable force. Actually, a hard reed vibrates less rapidly than a soft one. One can indeed produce a good tone with normal wind pressure and achieve adequate volume with a medium-soft or medium reed. In general, both extremely soft and extremely hard reeds should be avoided.

Handling Reeds. The season of the year should also be taken into account when dealing with reeds; that is, harder reeds are needed in the winter and softer reeds are usually required in the summer months. Choose a ligature that will enhance the vibrating qualities of the reed and not inhibit them. The ligature should be set about one-quarter of an inch below the line found on most mouthpieces. Its upper screw should be rather loose and its lower screw tightened just enough to hold the reed securely onto the mouthpiece.

A final cardinal principle that many clarinet players violate is the holding position of the instrument. Many clarinetists hold their instruments at a 45 (or more) degree angle from the body. To achieve a fuller, richer, and more flexible tone the clarinetist should sit (or stand) erect with the head up and the mouthpiece and instrument at considerably *less* than a 45 degree angle from the body. This, of course, is difficult to do at first, but the splendid results in terms of achieving a rich, flexible tone are well worth the time and effort involved. This position both allows the reed to vibrate more freely and increases the length of the reed's vibrating area. The study and improvement of clarinet tone quality is a goal that is never reached, but always strived for. (See Figure 6-B.)

Refining intonation on the clarinet

It would seem that the prime prerequisite for playing in tune is fine pitch sensitivity. If the clarinet student does not have this essential quality it is doubtful that he could ever be able to play well in tune. Obviously this is, to a greater or lesser degree, an innate talent which is part and parcel of the musician's tools. On the other hand it is sometimes painfully apparent that students who do have reasonably good pitch sensitivity have never been taught how to develop and use it. The business of listening carefully both when practicing alone and when playing in a group is extremely important. This skill cannot be developed overnight. Rather, it should be started during the student's first year of study. Donald Stauffer concludes that:

> There is definitely a need for more rigorous training of the listening process in the early experience of wind instrumentalists. There is good reason for an intonation consciousness to be fostered and developed right from the beginning.[2]

Daniel Bonade states:

> But even when our instrument and reed are satisfactory, the problem remains. The real cure, in the final analysis, lies only in listening carefully. If one does not concentrate on intonation while playing, it is impossible for him to play in tune.[3]

Surely a primary duty of a conscientious manufacturer is to provide the player with a correctly tuned instrument. Assuming that the clarinet student has both a first-line instrument (tuned to A-440 at 72 degrees Fahrenheit) and a first-line mouthpiece (which fits that instrument), he should also be aware of the fol-

---

[2]Donald W. Stauffer, *Intonation Deficiencies of Wind Instruments in Ensemble* (Washington, D.C.: The Catholic University of America Press, 1954), p. 183.
[3]Daniel Bonade, "Playing in Tune" *The Clarinet*, Winter, 1954–1955, p. 10.

lowing points. All clarinets must be both carefully and regularly
tuned to the standard international pitch of A-440. The unfortunate tendency for some groups to adopt a higher standard pitch
(even as high as A-445) causes a multitude of severe intonation
problems. The majority of instruments are simply not designed
to function well intonation-wise at this level of pitch. A much
better result can be achieved if a genuine effort is made to remain
at the A-440 level.

Tuning the Clarinet. It is recommended that the clarinet be
initially tuned in the following manner:

1. Play second line "g" and tune with the barrel joint. (In
   most cases the mouthpiece joint should not be used for
   tuning purposes.)
2. Play middle "c" and tune with the middle joint.
3. Play third line "b" and tune with the bell joint.

It is always wise to use tuning forks, tuning bars, or an electronic
instrument for tuning. Employment of a stroboscopic device for
developing and checking intonation is most valuable. The piano
is usually a poor tuning instrument since its pitch is easily affected
by temperature changes. Moreover, temperature affects the piano
and wind instruments in reverse directions; that is, a low temperature raises the piano's pitch while lowering the pitch of the wind
instruments and vice versa. When the barrel joint has been pulled
out tuning rings should be used. They are designed to fit into the
bottom of the barrel joint and will thus fill the gap created by
pulling out this joint in order to flatten the pitch of the clarinet.
Tuning rings are especially important in maintaining good intonation in the throat register. These rings are now available commercially at most music stores and can be purchased in sets of
several thicknesses.

Selecting Reeds. Playing on reeds which are either too hard or
too soft is yet another cause of faulty intonation. The soft reed
tends to play flat while the hard reed tends to play consistently
sharp. A reed of medium strength will give better results. Over-
size pads can contribute to intonation problems as well as to clarinet tone quality in general. It is amazing how much tone an over-
size pad located too near the tone-hole can absorb. Extremely
sensitive adjustments in tuning, such as underboring (enlarging

Figure 6–B   Playing Position for the Clarinet, Side View

the tone hole by the use of a reamer) or the use of shellac in the tone holes, should generally be assigned to a specialist in tuning clarinets. Unfortunately, there are only a limited number of people truly qualified for this highly skilled work.

Most manufacturers of clarinets make barrels of varying lengths. The important thing to keep in mind is that the bore of the barrel must match that of the clarinet on which it will be used. If the length of the barrel chosen is not drastically different from the standard length barrel, the overall tuning of the clarinet will probably not be greatly affected. The throat register is by far the most sensitive to change in barrel length and should be carefully considered when choosing a barrel.

It should be pointed out that the tuning of clarinets is at best a compromise. No manufacturer has yet made a clarinet perfectly in tune. When one stops to consider the many variables, such as physical differences of each clarinet student regarding embouchure, oral cavity size and lung cavity size, as well as temperature and humidity, it is amazing that intonation problems are not much more severe. Clearly, much knowledge, effort, concentration, and adjustment are necessary if the clarinet student hopes to cope effectively with the ever-present problem of playing his instrument in tune.

A selected and annotated list of clarinet solo literature for the development of specific individual skills

The purpose here is to single out a number of compositions which will aid in the development of specific musical performance skills on many levels of student development. These skills might include such technical and musical problems as coordination of tongue and fingers, phrasing, articulation, legato playing, breath control, and technique. There are also brief comments regarding the solos per se, their level of difficulty, and their accompaniments.

Arnold, *Sonatina for Clarinet and Pianoforte* (Mills). This contemporary English work is lively, witty, and generally charming. It is a very musical solo and one that is well suited for the development of technique, phrasing, and breath control. Both clarinet and piano parts are on the advanced level and the last movement is especially tricky rhythmically.

Barlow, *Lyrical Piece* (Carl Fischer). This is an excellent solo for the study of tone quality. Technically, it is not too demanding, but some rhythmic problems are present. The accompaniment is quite difficult, while the clarinet part is on the medium-advanced level.

Becker-Voxman, *Romance* (Rubank). An effective solo for the less advanced high school player, this work is particularly good for the development of phrasing. With the exception of the cadenza there are no great technical demands. The accompaniment is easy.

Bergson-Voxman, *Scene and Air* (Rubank). This is a good, moderately advanced solo for the development of cadenza interpretation and phrasing. The final section is especially helpful in developing good coordination between tongue and fingers as well as a clean, light, and crisp staccato. The accompaniment is not too demanding.

Brahms, *Sonatas 1 and 2* (Carl Fischer). Both of these sonatas are major works in the repertory of the clarinet and require a musically mature clarinetist and pianist for performance. They are excellent for the development of all aspects of musicianship with the possible exception of technique. The clarinet parts are not too demanding technically but the piano parts definitely require an advanced pianist both technically and musically.

Cavallini, *Adagio e Tarantella* (Cundy-Bettoney). The *Adagio* section of this solo provides the moderately advanced clarinet student with much opportunity for the development of rubato and recitative playing. There are many changes of style and mood in this solo and a good technical command of the instrument is a must for a convincing interpretation. The accompaniment is not particularly difficult.

Debussy, *Premiere Rhapsodie* (Elkan-Vogel). Every advanced clarinetist should study and perform this work. It is particularly good for the development of accurate rhythm, expressive phrasing, precise technique, coordination of tongue and fingers, and a clean, light staccato. An advanced pianist is required for the accompaniment.

Finzi, *Five Bagatelles* (Boosey & Hawkes). All five compositions are excellent music and range in difficulty from easy to advanced. The *Prelude* (moderately advanced) is good for the development of smooth phrasing and legato tonguing. The *Romance* is helpful in the development of breath control and smooth legato-type playing. It is not difficult technically, and its accompaniment does not require an advanced pianist. The *Carol* makes fine material for the less advanced high school clarinet student. It is particularly well written for the development of tone quality, dynamics, and a light attack. The accompaniment is also not difficult. The *Forlana* is a little more difficult than the *Carol*. It is very good for the development of phrasing and dynamics. The

Fughetta is the most advanced of all five works and requires both a clarinet student of considerable skill as well as a fine accompanist. It is especially good for the development of clean, precise execution and rapid, accurate technique.

Guilhaud, *First Concertino* (Carl Fischer). This fine French solo is most effective for either contest or recital. It provides good opportunity for the development of style in cadenza playing, and its *Allegretto* section is excellent for the development of a light, brisk staccato. Its slow sections stress tone quality and phrasing. The accompaniment is not too demanding, but the solo part requires a moderately advanced clarinetist.

Honegger, *Sonatine* (Rouart Lerolle). *Sonatine* is comprised of three short movements, the third being in the jazz idiom. This is a very good work and one that is most interesting and enjoyable to play and perform. The final movement does, however, pose some rhythmic problems for both clarinet and piano. Advanced students on both instruments are required.

Mazellier-Waln, *Fantasy-Ballet* (Neil Kjos). This brilliant French art solo is excellent for the development of musical interpretation as well as the building of technique on the clarinet. Musically and technically it is on the advanced level. Several sections require the use of alternate fingering patterns. The accompaniment is also on the advanced level.

Mozart, *Concerto for Clarinet in Bb*, K. 622 (Carl Fischer). This work is regarded by many authorities as the greatest composition written for the clarinet. Every mature clarinetist should study and perform it. Technically, it is not too demanding. Because of this, unfortunately, the Mozart *Concerto* is too often performed by students who clearly lack the musical maturity to perform it. This concerto is especially good for the development of smooth, flawless technique (first movement), breath control and expressive phrasing (second movement), and precision of technical execution in the final movement. The accompaniment has been revised from the original orchestral score and is on the moderately advanced level.

Mozart-Bellison, *Divertimento in Bb* (G. Ricordi Co.). This is a very euphonic and pleasing solo for the less advanced high school clarinetist. Technically, neither clarinet part nor piano accompaniment is difficult. It is, however, a very musical solo and very good for the development of the student's overall musicianship.

Saint-Säens, *Sonata for Clarinet and Piano* (Elkan-Vogel). This is one of the composer's best sonatas and is interesting and enjoyable to study and perform. A moderately advanced clarinetist and pianist are required. The first movement lends itself well to the development of phrasing, the second movement for precise, smooth finger coordination, the third movement for dynamic contrast and breath control, and the final movement for rapid and accurate technical execution.

Schumann-Simon, *Fantasy-Pieces* (G. Schirmer). One of the truly fine works for clarinet and piano, this composition is excellent for the development of overall musicianship. Both pianist and clarinetist must be musically sensitive performers. *Fantasy-Pieces* is a very good work for developing tone quality, phrasing, breath control, and expressive dynamics. The piano part is quite difficult.

Spohr, *Concertos 1 and 2* (Cundy-Bettoney). These concertos make very effective study material for the advanced clarinetist. They are especially good for the development of rapid and fluent technique. The piano accompaniments have been revised from the original orchestral scores and are on the moderately advanced level. These works were written in the same general idiom as the Weber *Concertos* but are more demanding technically.

Verhey-Voxman, *Nocturne* (Rubank). *Nocturne* is a fine solo for developing breath control and expressive phrasing. A wide range of the instrument is also covered in this work. The accompaniment is not difficult and the clarinet part is on the moderately advanced level.

Weber, *Grand Duo Concertant* (G. Schirmer). This work is believed by many to be Weber's finest composition for the clarinet. It is an especially good number for the development of ensemble playing (in this case between clarinet and piano.). The second movement requires excellent breath control and phrasing. Both the first and third movements stress the development of clean, precise technique and there are numerous passages which require fine coordination between tongue and fingers. The clarinet part is on the advanced level. The piano part of this duet is particularly demanding.

Selected bibliography

Ayres, Thomas A., "Clarinet Choir Literature," *The Instrumentalist*, vol. 18, April, 1964, p. 83.

Bonade, Daniel, *The Clarinetist's Compendium*. Kenosha, Wisconsin: Leblanc Publications, Inc., 1962.

Cailliet, Lucien, *The Clarinet and Clarinet Choir*. Kenosha, Wisconsin: Leblanc Publications, Inc., 1955.

Cailliet, Lucien, "The Clarinet Choir," *Woodwind World*, vol. 5, February, 1964, p. 6.

Cailliet, Lucien, "The Role of the Contrabass Clarinet," *The World of Music*, vol. 10, Fall, 1963, p. 10.

Eby, W., *The Clarinet Embouchure*. New York: Walter Jacobs Co., 1927.

Heim, Norman M., *A Handbook for Clarinet Performance*, Leblanc Publications, Inc., 1967.

Howland, Russell S., "The Clarinet Choir—Its Development and Use," *The Instrumentalist*, vol. 18, November, 1963, p. 78.

Jennings, Vance, "The Clarinet Choir Movement," *National Association of College Wind and Percussion Instructors Bulletin*, vol. 11, March, 1963, p. 4.

McCathren, Donald, *Playing and Teaching the Clarinet Family*. San Antonio, Texas: Southern Music Company, 1959.

Opperman, K., *Handbook for Making and Adjusting Single Reeds*. New York: Chappel & Company, 1956.

Opperman, K., *Repertory of the Clarinet*. New York: G. Ricordi & Company, 1960.

Rasmussen, Mary and Mattran, Donald, *A Teacher's Guide to the Literature of Woodwind Instruments*. Durham, New Hampshire: Appleyard Publications, 1966.

Reed, Alfred, *The Balanced Clarinet Choir*. Kenosha, Wisconsin: Leblanc Publications, Inc., 1958.

Rendall, F., *The Clarinet, Some Notes Upon Its History and Construction*. New York: Philosophical Library, 1954.

Stein, Keith, *The Art of Clarinet Playing*. Evanston, Illinois: Summy-Birchard Co., 1958.

Stubbins, W. H., *The Art of Clarinetistry*, Ann Arbor, Michigan: Ann Arbor Publishers, 1965.

Thurston, F., *Clarinet Technique*. London: Oxford University Press, 1956.

Timm, E., *The Woodwinds*. Boston: Allyn Bacon, 1964.

Tose, Gabriel, *Artistic Clarinet Technique and Study*. Hollywood, California: Highland Music Co., 1962.

Weerts, Richard, "The Contrabass Clarinet in the Modern Symphonic Band," *The Instrumentalist*, vol. 4, November, 1964, p. 47.

Westphal, Frederick W., *Guide to Teaching Woodwinds*, Dubuque, Iowa: Wm. C. Brown Company, 1962.

Willaman, Robert, *The Clarinet and Clarinet Playing*. New York: Carl Fischer, Inc., 1949.

CHAPTER 7

The Bassoon

A recent article points out that:

> There are still many high school bands which do not have
> bassoons, or have poor bassoons, because the director has
> never had the opportunity of really learning the problems
> involved in this instrument. As a result, there is a tendency
> to shy away from purchasing them or, if the school already
> owns bassoons, there is a reluctance to start pupils.[1]

Actually, of course, the bassoon can and should be an important
member of high school bands and orchestras. The purpose here
is to acquaint the reader with many important facets of bassoon
performance and teaching which will aid in the development of
the bassoonist for the high school band.

Selecting instructional materials

The amount of instructional materials written particularly for
the bassoon is somewhat limited when compared to similar materials written for the other woodwinds. Because of this situation
it has long been the practice of bassoon instructors to make ex-

---

[1]Harold Palmer, "Bassoon Fundamentals," *The Insrtumentalist*, January, 1967,
p. 50.

tensive use of both trombone and cello materials. When carefully selected and adapted these materials can be used to great advantage by the bassoonist. Since the bassoon student is frequently started on the secondary level, beginning methods are listed for this instrument.

Beginning Methods

Elementary Method for Bassoon .... Skornicka-Rubank
Elementary Method for Bassoon .... Buck-Neil A. Kjos
A Tune a Day for Bassoon .... Herfurth-Stuart,
                                                   Boston Music Co.

Intermediate Methods

Intermediate Method for Bassoon .... Voxman-Rubank
Practical Method for Bassoon .... Weissenborn-Carl Fischer
Advanced Method for Bassoon (two volumes) .... Voxman-
                                                   Gower, Rubank
Method for Bassoon, Book II .... Fields-Cole

Medium Advanced Methods

Jancourt Bassoon Studies .... Collins-Belwin
Forty Progressive Etudes, Book I .... Lee-Carl Fischer
(a cello book well adapted to the bassoon)
60 Studies for Bassoon (two volumes) .... Kovar-Kopprasch,
                                                   International

Advanced Etudes

25 Studies in All Keys .... Milde-Cundy Bettoney
Concert Studies, Books I and II .... Milde-Cundy Bettoney
20 Studies for Bassoon .... Vaulet-Rubank
18 Studies .... Gambaro-International

Choosing a bassoon, student adaptability, bassoon recordings, and care of the bassoon

A "Heckel system" bassoon is recommended since this system is generally considered to be standard in the United States. Any bassoon under consideration for purchase should have a "whisper key," a great aid in producing nearly half of the notes on the bassoon. Essentially, this key functions in reverse to the octave key on the clarinets; that is, it is employed to achieve many of the low notes on the bassoon. The first of the lower tones to be aided by the use of the whisper key is fourth line "F" in the bass clef. The instrument should also be equipped with at least two bocals of different lengths for the purpose of tuning. A used bassoon should be carefully checked by a competent person for such items as cracked bocals, chipped edges and rotted wood around the tone holes, pads in poor condition, and loose posts.

The Bassoon Player. The bassoon, like the oboe, is not normally a "beginning" instrument. The prospective bassoonist should have had previous musical experience on the piano and another woodwind instrument if possible. It is also wise to select a fine student academically and one who has a strong desire to play the bassoon. Physically, the student should have fairly large hands with long fingers. Even front teeth are also an asset. Fine pitch sensitivity is not only desirable but essential.

The following recordings are suggested for use in demonstrating the bassoon:

> "The Instruments of the Orchestra" (with narrator and performed by first desk men of the Vienna State Opera Orchestra), Vanguard Records #VRS-1017 and VRS-1018.
>
> "Concert Piece for Bassoon and String Orchestra" by Burrill Phillips. Sol Schoenbach, Bassoonist. Columbia #ML 4629.
>
> "Leonard Sharrow Bassoon Solos," Coronet Recording Co., Columbus, Ohio. Program LP #1294.
>
> "Sonata for Bassoon and Piano" by Paul Hindemith. Bernard Garfield, Bassoonist. EMS Record #EMS 4.
>
> "Concerto in B♭, K. 191" by W. A. Mozart. Leonard Sharrow, Bassoonist. RCA-Victor #LM-1030.

Caring for the Bassoon. The bassoon, like most musical instruments, is a very delicate mechanism and requires the best of care at all times. The following general comments can be made regarding care of the bassoon. In most cases the inside of the bore should not be oiled since the majority of bassoons are now either rubber lined in part or specially treated to resist moisture. The key mechanism should be oiled occasionally with a high grade fine oil. The instrument should be cleaned both inside and out every time it is used. A chamois or soft cloth can be used for the outside and swabs are normally provided by the manufacturer for the inside. The crook (mouthpipe) can be cleaned by running warm water through it periodically. It should be noted that the small hole in the neb of the whisper key will probably need to be opened frequently. A straw from a whisk broom can be used for this purpose. The crook is quite expensive and easily damaged. Special care and protection should be given this important part of the bassoon.

Detailed instructions for the care of the bassoon are available from any manufacturer. Much time, energy, and money (not to mention frustration) will be saved if these instructions are carefully studied and then practiced by the bassoonist.

Teaching bassoon playing

When considering the problem of embouchure on the bassoon the following points should be observed. The lips should be "bunched" toward the center and should seem to *encircle* the reed rather than clamp from top to bottom in a vise-like manner. Pressure should be applied *all around* the reed instead of on the top and bottom only. The lower jaw should be dropped down and back as suggested in Figure 7-A. The lower lip should be about

Figure 7–A

one-half inch behind the upper lip as a result of moving the lower jaw down and back. (See Figure 7-A.)

Tones and Reeds. A medium strength reed is recommended even for beginning students since a reed that is too soft will offer little or no resistance and therefore militate against the development of the embouchure. On the other hand, a reed that is too hard will usually prove to be exceedingly difficult for a beginner to use. The embouchure should be developed slowly. It will tire quickly at first. Thus frequent practice periods are suggested for short periods of time until the embouchure has had a chance to develop. (See Figure 7-B.)

Two ways for a student to get a conception of a good tone on the bassoon are: (1) to listen to an excellent bassoonist in live performance, and (2) to listen to excellent bassoon recordings. It is possible for a teacher to describe a pleasing sound on the bassoon, but a much better result can be achieved if he is able to perform, to some extent at least, for the student. Both tone and intonation depend largely on the degree of pitch sensitivity inherent in the student, the quality of the bassoon, and the quality and condition of the reed. Ideally, of course, the student should be taught to construct his own reeds by a competent bassoonist skilled in this craft. If this is not possible he should find a satisfactory reed source and stay with it.

Bocal Lengths of the Bassoon. The different length bocals are of some help in improving intonation on the bassoon. Normally, bocals come in various lengths and are numbered—the lower the number the shorter the length. The numbering is usually from one to three. The shorter bocals are used to *raise* the pitch of the bassoon and, conversely, the longer bocals are used to *lower* the pitch. Alternate fingerings are also employed to either raise or lower the pitch of given tones. There is no substitute, however, for a first-line bassoon built relatively well in tune *within itself* and a bassoonist with fine pitch sensitivity as well as a good concept of an idiomatic bassoon tone. In terms of intonation the bassoon is probably more capricious than any other woodwind instrument. This is partly because of its shape and size and partly due to the fact that some of its holes must be bored at an angle to make it possible for the player's fingers to cover them.

Adjusting bassoon reeds

The following tools are listed as a minimum requirement for working with bassoon reeds:

1. Long nose small pliers
2. Reamer
3. Folding knife
4. Sharpening stone
5. Bassoon plaque
6. Bassoon mandrel (to hold the reed while adjusting it)
7. Small hard wood block (for cutting tips of the reeds)
8. A number of "rough" or "unfinished" bassoon reeds to experiment on.

Often it is not necessary to use a knife on a reed, but merely to adjust the wire or wires as the case may be. The two visible wires on the reed (see Figure 7-C) function inversely to each other; that is, if the front wire is pressed (from top to bottom) the tip of the reed will *close*. If the second wire is pressed in the same manner (from top to bottom) the tip of the reed will *open*. In general, the opening at the tip of the reed should be approximately one-sixteenth of an inch. Opening the tip of the reed will give it more resistance, thus causing it to play harder. Closing the tip will decrease the reed's resistance thus making it a softer reed. As is the case with all reeds, single and double, hard reeds tend to play sharp in pitch, whereas soft ones tend to play flat.

The Soft Reed. If a reed is too soft and offers little resistance, the first procedure is to open the tip by adjusting the front wire. (In the event that the front wire does not function properly the tip may be opened by adjusting the second wire.) If the reed is still too soft a small portion should be cut from the tip using the knife and hard wood block. Care should be taken to secure a clean, even cut. Only a small portion should be trimmed from the tip since additional amounts may be taken off later if required.

The Hard Reed. If a reed is too hard first try to close slightly its tip in the manner indicated previously. If the reed is still too hard it probably will require trimming. Before trimming a reed, or making any adjustment on it, it should be soaked in tap water for about five minutes. The *mandrel* functions to hold the reed

Figure 7—B **Bassoon Embouchure and Hand Position**

while adjusting it. The tip of the reed should be held below the rim of a desk lamp in order to tell (by the light and dark areas) where the reed is too heavy or too thin. The *plaque* should be kept between the blades of the reed while working on it in order to protect the tip and under half of the reed. Trim all surfaces equally while being careful *not* to trim the "C" (heart) area very much. When the heart area is too thin, as tends to be the case with most commercially made bassoon reeds, the reed will cave in and offer almost no resistance to the embouchure. This will result in both a very poor tone quality and faulty intonation.

Not all bassoon reeds can be trimmed in the same way because of their different shapes and constructions. Generally, a reed should be uniform; that is, it should be light throughout. It is a good policy to have the center back (area "C") slightly darker or thicker than the other parts of the reed. The knife should not be used too rigorously as it will cut the reed too fast and possibly ruin it. Always work slowly and make changes slight and even. (See Figure 7-C)[2]

Often the low tones will respond more easily if the back (A and B) areas are thinned out slightly. The front of the reed helps govern and control the high notes and, by thinning a heavy tip, more accurate tonguing will result. The thickness of the tip of each blade varies with the strength of the cane, but it should be approximately as thick as the plaque. If trouble is experienced with leakage where the reed fits onto the crook, about one-half inch of the dry reed should be held in hot melted beeswax. This will fill the small crevices. After cooling, the surplus wax should be trimmed away and when it is fitted (reed to crook) the reed will be nearly leakproof. One dipping is usually sufficient for the life of the reed.

Practicing with Reeds. A great deal of practice on old reeds is strongly recommended before attempting to adjust new ones. Although the basic skills can be taught and numerous books have been written on the subject, the fact remains that *logical experimentation,* or the "trial and error" method, is probably the best way to find out how to work with and adjust bassoon reeds.

---

[2]Adapted from *Guide to Teaching Woodwinds* by Frederick W. Westphal. Used by permission of Wm. C. Brown Company Publishers.

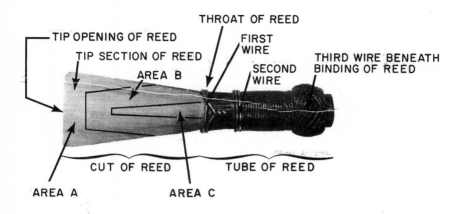

THROAT OF REED

TIP OPENING OF REED   FIRST WIRE

TIP SECTION OF REED

AREA B   SECOND WIRE

THIRD WIRE BENEATH BINDING OF REED

CUT OF REED   TUBE OF REED

AREA A   AREA C

Figure 7–C

The life of a good reed tends to vary tremendously. Among the factors involved are how much the reed is used, the quality of the reed's cane, the season of the year (normally reeds perform better and last longer in the warm, humid months than in the winter), the care the reed receives, and the chemical make-up of the player's saliva. Many players are successful in prolonging the life span of their reeds by obtaining three of four good reeds at a time and then alternating them. Once a reed ceases to function in a satisfactory manner it should be discarded. Too many woodwind players are guilty of playing on reeds that are no longer functional. In general, the care of the bassoon reed is similar to that of the oboe reed described in Chapter 8.

Using vibrato

Most authorities appear to be in concurrence that a pleasing and musical vibrato is essential to the bassoon tone. They also seem to agree that the best method for achieving a vibrato is by employing the diaphragm instead of either the throat or jaw methods. The fundamental aspects of the diaphragm vibrato are described in Chapter 8, "The Oboe." Spencer feels that "most talented students who are told to 'make the sound sing' can find the necessary muscular action without any special instruction."[3] Clearly, however, most bassoon students will probably require skilled help as they attempt to develop vibratos. There is, of course, no substitute for private instruction by a competent bassoonist. If this is not available, much can be learned by listening to fine recordings.

A great deal of difficulty is nearly always experienced if vibrato is attempted too early in the student's development. It is essential that he have a fairly solid foundation on the instrument in terms of a good straight tone quality, good embouchure, and a reasonable amount of technique before commencing with the study of vibrato. Finally, it should always be remembered that vibrato cannot be construed to be a panacea for a basically poor tone quality and/or faulty intonation. It can only enhance and embellish a good straight tone quality and fundamentally good intonation.

A selected and annotated list of bassoon solo literature for the development of specific individual skills

Benson, *Song and Dance* (Boosey & Hawkes). *Song and Dance* is one of the fine easy solos for the young bassoonist. It is written in the modern idiom. Although the demands on the bassoonist are limited, it is a very interesting solo which the student should enjoy. The accompaniment is easy.

Cohen, *Danse Grotesque* (Belwin). On the moderately advanced level, this solo should prove to be both interesting and challenging to the young bassoonist. Its accompaniment is easy and the solo part remains in the bass clef. This is a good solo for developing coordination of tongue and fingers as well as staccato facility on the instrument.

Dunhill, *Lyric Suite* (Boosey & Hawkes). This suite consists of five movements. All are scored in the bass clef and are not too demanding in terms of key signatures and ranges. Technically, the accompani-

---

[3]William Spencer, *The Art of Bassoon Playing* (Evanston: Summy-Birchard Company, 1958), p. 51.

ments seem to be more demanding than the solo parts. *Lyric Suite* is good repertory material for the development of the moderately advanced bassoonist. Areas of performance stressed are compound rhythm, development of both staccato and legato playing, coordination of tongue and fingers, and musical phrasing.

Etler, *Sonata for Bassoon and Piano* (Associated). This is a well-written, moderately contemporary work. It should be of more than casual interest for the serious bassoonist. An overall fine modern sonata for the development of the intellectually-minded advanced bassoonist and pianist.

Garfield, *Soliloquy* (Edition Musicus). A fine solo for the young bassoonist, *Soliloquy* was composed by the first bassoonist of the Philadelphia Orchestra. The accompaniment is not difficult. This is a good solo for the development of breath control and legato playing. A short passage will serve to introduce the student to the tenor clef.

Hindemith, *Sonata for Bassoon and Piano* (Associated). This is one of Hindemith's better efforts in the area of instrumental sonatas. It is a genuinely musical work and should be in the repertory of every bassoonist. It is excellent for the study and development of nearly every aspect of musical performance on the bassoon. This sonata is on the advanced level and requires an excellent pianist.

Jancourt, *Reverie* (Cundy-Bettoney). *Reverie* is a moderately advanced solo and can be used to advantage in the study and development of various ornamental figures such as trills, grace notes, and turns. There are several changes of tempo and mood, as well as a brief cadenza. This solo should provide the student bassoonist with good material for the development of interpretation and musical phrasing. The accompaniment is technically more difficult than the solo part.

Moffat and Rapp, *Old Master Melodies for Young Cellists* (Schott). The collection of twelve easy compositions is excellent material for the neophyte bassoonist of any age. Included are works by Weber, Mozart, Telemann, Corelli and others. The accompaniments are not excessively difficult. Both key signatures and ranges of the solo parts are limited. This collection is especially good for the development of tone quality as well as the study of interpretation and phrasing.

Mozart, *Concerto in Bb Major*, K. 191 (Baron). This Mozart bassoon concerto is probably the best known and most frequently performed of all bassoon concertos. Every advanced bassoonist should have it in his repertory. Technically, it is not too demanding. The bassoonist should have a considerable degree of musical maturity, however, before he studies this work. It is excellent for both the technical as well as the musical development of the bassoonist.

Phillips, *Concert Piece* (Carl Fischer). *Concert Piece* is an appealing work that is a favorite with advanced bassoonists. The opening and closing sections are quite brilliant and the lyrical middle section involves reading in the tenor clef. With the exception of the final run this solo is only moderately difficult technically. It was originally written for bassoon and strings. The piano reduction is effective but requires an excellent pianist for performance.

Rossler, *Concerto in Bb Major* (Schott). This concerto was written approximately during the time of Mozart. All three movements are scored in the bass clef. The *Adagio* (second movement) is particularly good for the development of legato playing, phrasing, and interpretation. Both bassoon and piano parts are on the moderately difficult level. This work should be studied prior to the Mozart *Concerto*.

Schmutz, *Melodie Lyrique* (Belwin). Although written in a comparatively easy key and without excessive demands in terms of range, *Melodie Lyrique* is good material for the study and execution of various rhythmic figures as well as development of legato playing. No tenor clef is involved, and both solo and accompaniment parts are on the moderately easy level.

Stevens, *Three Pieces* (Peters). This is a comparatively recent work by an American composer of considerable repute. It is written in the modern idiom and is well scored for the bassoon and piano. *Three Pieces* is particularly good for the study and development of rhythm. Some reading in the tenor clef is involved. Both bassoon and piano parts are on the advanced level.

Vivaldi, *Sonata in A Minor* (International). This is a most idiomatically written sonata for the bassoon. A considerable degree of sheer endurance is required when it is performed in its entirety. The tenor clef is used extensively. A great deal of ornamentation is also found in this work. In general, the Vivaldi *Sonata in A Minor* is a good work for the development of the advanced bassoonist. An excellent pianist is also required.

Weber, *Concerto in F Major*, Opus 75 (Cundy-Bettoney). This is a rather lengthy concerto. The final movement, *Rondo*, is probably the most exciting, both musically and technically. It is a brilliant movement in the typical Weber style and very good for the development of fluent and precise technique on the bassoon. An advanced bassoonist is required. The accompaniment is not excessively demanding.

Weissenborn, *Capriccio* (Cundy-Bettoney). This fast-moving solo is good for the development of technical facility and expanding the range of the moderately advanced bassoonist. The accompaniment is easy. The solo part is written entirely in the bass clef. There are a few relatively awkward passages in terms of fingerings and wide-range slurs.

Seventy-six Bassoon Solos (Belwin). Good material for the beginning bassoonist. This collection is very limited in terms of demands on the bassoonist's technique, range, and overall knowledge of music and the instrument. Yet it provides numerous solos which are interesting, challenging, and good for his development. The accompaniments are usually not difficult.

Selected bibliography

Camden, Archie, *Bassoon Technique*. New York: Oxford University Press, 1962.

Christlieb, Donald, "Bassoon Reeds, Their Design, Construction, and Measurement," (Part I) *National Association of College Wind and Percussion Instructors Bulletin*, vol. 13, Winter, 1965, p. 20.

Christlieb, Donald, "Bassoon Reeds, Their Design, Construction, and Measurement," (Part II) *National Association of College Wind and Percussion Instructors Bulletin*, vol. 13, Spring, 1965, p. 21.

Christlieb, Donald, "Bassoon Reeds, Their Design, Construction, and Measurement," (Part III) *National Association of College Wind and Percussion Instructors Bulletin*, vol. 13, Summer, 1965, p. 19.

Echols, Gary, "Solo and Ensemble Literature for Bassoon," *The Instrumentalist*, vol. 28, September, 1963, p. 91.

Fox, Hugo, *Let's Play Bassoon*. South Whitley, Indiana: Fox Bassoon Company, 1961.

Heckel, Wilhelm, "The Bassoon" (translated by Thomas C. Collins) Part I. *National Association of College Wind and Percussion Instructors Bulletin*, vol. 10, December, 1961, p. 11.

Heckel, Wilhelm, "The Bassoon" (translated by Thomas C. Collins) Part II. *National Association of College Wind and Percussion Instructors Bulletin*, vol. 10, March, 1962, p. 10.

Heckel, Wilhelm, "The Bassoon" (translated by Thomas C. Collins) Part III. *National Association of College Wind and Percussion Instructors Bulletin*, vol. 10, June, 1962, p. 14.

Heckel, Wilhelm, "The Bassoon" (translated by Thomas C. Collins) Part IV. *National Association of College Wind and Percussion Instructors Bulletin*, vol. 11, September, 1962, p. 11.

Organ, Robert J., *The Bassoon, Performance—Teaching*. Denver, Colorado: Rebo Publications, 1954.

Palmer, Harold, "Bassoon Fundamentals," *The Instrumentalist*, vol. 21, January, 1967, p. 50.

Pence, Homer, *Teacher's Guide to the Bassoon*. Elkhart, Indiana: H. & A. Selmer, Inc., 1963.

Schleiffer, J. Eric, "The Bassoon: Three Technical Studies," *Music Educators Journal*, vol. 53, January, 1967, p. 57.

Spencer, William, *The Art of Bassoon Playing*. Evanston, Illinois: Summy-Birchard Publishing Company, 1958.

Spencer, William, "Bassoon Vibrato," *The Instrumentalist*, vol. 19, February, 1965, p. 77.

Waln, Ronald E., "Solo Literature for the Bassoon," *The Instrumentalist*, vol. 15, October, 1961, p. 80.

Westphal, Frederick W., *Guide to Teaching Woodwinds*. Dubuque, Iowa: Wm. C. Brown Company, 1962.

CHAPTER 8

The Oboe

Many believe that the oboe was the instrument around which the woodwind section was developed. Actually, the history of the oboe can be traced to the thirteenth century as it descended from the shawm. Many improvements have been incorporated into this instrument, especially during the mid and late nineteenth century. Basically, however, the oboe reached its present-day form in the mid-seventeenth century in France. The oboe is, by its very nature, a solo instrument. It is a conspicuous and important member of both school bands and orchestras.

Selecting instructional materials

The available instructional material for the oboe is not as abundant as for some of the other instruments. This appears to be especially the case on the lower levels of development. More instructional material is available for the moderately advanced and advanced student. Since the oboist is frequently started on the secondary level beginning methods are listed for this instrument.

Beginning Methods

Rubank Elementary Method	Hovey-Rubank
Basic Method for the Oboe	Carey-Carl Fischer
Gekeler Method, Book I	Belwin

Intermediate Methods

Niemann-Labate Method, Book I	Carl Fischer
Rubank Intermediate Method (Skornicka-Koebner)	Rubank
Gekeler Method, Book II	Belwin

Medium Advanced Methods

Gekeler Method, Book III .... Belwin
Advanced Method for Oboe (Two Volumes) .... Rubank
Niemann-Labate Method, Book II .... Carl Fischer

Advanced Methods

Selected Studies (Voxman) .... Rubank
16 Daily Exercises for Oboe (Tabate) .... Carl Fischer
27 Virtuoso Studies for Oboe (Bassi) .... Carl Fischer
Vade-Mecum for the Oboist .... Andraud-Southern Music Co.
William D. Fitch Oboe Method .... George Wahr,
(This is an especially good method   Ann Arbor, Mich.
    for students with a background on
    another instrument)
Technical Studies (Tustin) .... Peer International

Choosing an oboe, student adaptability, oboe recordings, and care of the oboe

Although oboes are quite expensive, it is recommended that only first-line, full plateau conservatory system models be purchased. These closed hole models are significantly more satisfactory than the simplified conservatory models with open rings. It is also suggested that the oboe have two single-effect (not automatic) octave keys and a low Bb. If possible the oboe should be checked by an experienced oboist for pitch and even quality of blowing before it is purchased. In addition to a general evaluation of the instrument, Robert Sprenkle and David Ledet indicate that special attention should be given to the following specific points:

1. Quality of tone
2. General pitch level
3. Relative intonation
4. Uniformity of response
5. Stability: that is, if the oboe sags or gurgles on some notes.[1]

Three Points in Caring for the Oboe. When choosing a student for the oboe the following points should be kept in mind:

---

[1]Robert Sprenkle and David Ledet, *The Art of Oboe Playing* (Evanston: Summy-Birchard Company, 1961), p. 5.

1. The student should have a non-protruding lower jaw. Actually, a slightly receding lower jaw is advantageous.
2. He should be a fine student academically and an aggressive player with enthusiasm, drive, and perseverance. A piano background is helpful.
3. The student must possess good pitch sensitivity. Prior performance ability on another woodwind instrument, such as the clarinet, is most helpful. Even front teeth are also beneficial.

The following recordings can be used to demonstrate the oboe:

"The Instruments of the Orchestra" (with narrator and performed by first desk men of the Vienna State Opera Orchestra), Vanguard, records #VRS-1017 and VRS-1018.

"Concerto #3 in G Minor for Oboe and Strings" by Handel. Marcel Tabuteau, Oboist. Columbia #ML 4629.

"The Philadelphia Woodwind Quintet." John de Lancie, Oboist. Columbia #ML 5093.

"Boston Woodwind Quintet" (Concert at the Library of Congress) Ralph Gomberg, Oboist. Boston Record, #B-407.

"Oboe Recital." Patricia Stenberg, Oboist and Lowell Roddenberry, Pianist. Golden Crest Records, 220 Broadway, Huntington Station, New York.

Instructions and Major Repairs. The oboe is a very delicate mechanism and demands the best care at all times. When in need of major repair work it should be taken to a highly skilled woodwind specialist. As is the case with all musical instruments, proper care can prevent a great deal of repair work which is usually quite costly and time consuming. Virtually all oboe manufacturing firms provide complete instructions regarding the care and maintenance of the instrument. Clearly, these instructions should be studied by both instructor and student. First-line oboes can be played for long periods of time with only minor repairs, in most cases, if they receive proper care. Most authorities recommend a complete overhaul every one or two years, depending on the amount of use the instrument receives, the quality of the oboe, and the care rendered it.

Teaching oboe playing

The oboist's posture should be erect (but not rigid) with the chest up in order to free the lungs and the diaphragm for proper breathing. The player's head should be held up, similar to that of the clarinet player. The oboist's head and chin should *not* be tilted downward. The instrument itself should be held at approximately a 45 degree angle from the body and the fingers should be slightly arched. The wrists should be straight and the elbows held away from the body. The thumb rest should be on the base of the thumbnail.

Forming Oboe Embouchure. Basically, the following recommendations should be observed in the formation of a good oboe embouchure. The upper lip should be pulled down, covering the upper teeth, and the lower lip pulled well over the lower teeth until the red of the lower lip disappears. The corners of the mouth should be pulled *in* and pressure should be applied cautiously from *all around* the reed rather than on the top and bottom only. The student should be encouraged to use only as much pressure as is needed to control the reed. A medium strength reed is recommended even for beginning students. It should be noted that too little reed in the mouth tends to produce a flat pitch and a soggy tone quality, whereas too much reed tends to produce a pitch that is sharp and a tone that is harsh. The embouchure must be developed slowly. It will tire quickly at first. Thus frequent practice periods are suggested for short periods of time. (See Figure 8-A.)

As is the case with most other wind instruments, the oboe student should be taught from the onset to start all tones with his tongue and to tongue many notes with one steady column of air. The student should be taught to stop the tone by simply stopping the flow of air.

Oboe Tone and Intonation. Achieving a good tone and good intonation on the oboe are interrelated problems. As indicated previously, the oboe student must possess a fine degree of pitch sensitivity. In addition, he must have a clear concept of what a good oboe tone should sound like and how to achieve this sound. This can be accomplished in the following manner. The instructor should, if possible, demonstrate to the student by actual performance. If this is not feasible the student should be encouraged

Figure 8–A **Oboe Embouchure and Hand Position**

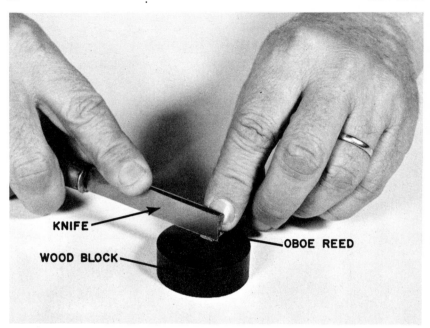

Figure 8–B

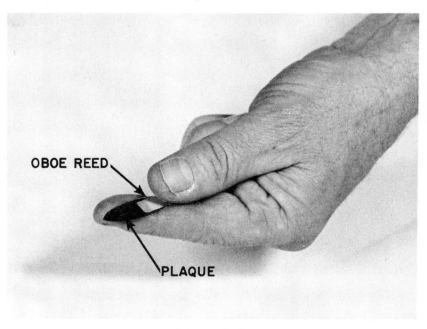

Figure 8–C

to listen to a competent performer on the oboe. If this is not possible he can learn much about developing a good oboe tonal concept by listening to recordings of this instrument.

In addition, the development of tone quality and intonation depends to a large degree on the quality of the reed and instrument. Ideally, the student should be taught to make his own reeds by a person knowledgeable in this art. If this cannot be arranged he should be encouraged to find a satisfactory reed source and stay with it. This will also be helpful in the development of the student's embouchure. Reeds which are flat in pitch should be shortened by cutting a bit from the tip. The sides of the reed can be made smooth by using dry Dutch rush or fine sandpaper. A reed which is sharp in pitch should be carefully scraped down. All adjustments on double reeds should be approached with caution since a perfectly good reed can be ruined by a stroke of the knife.

Adjusting oboe reeds

The following tools are listed as minimum requirements for working with oboe reeds:

1. Long nose small pliers
2. Folding knife
3. Sharpening stone
4. Oboe plaque
5. Oboe mandrel (to hold reed while adjusting it)
6. Small hard wood block (for cutting tips of the reeds)
7. A number of "rough" or "unfinished" oboe reeds to experiment on.

The new reed should be soaked in water for about ten minutes and then blown until it responds well. It should next be put on the oboe and played to find out if it is too soft or too hard. If the reed is too *soft*, hold it flat on the cutting block with the left hand and clip the reed straight across the tip edge. In order to insure a clean cut make certain that the knife is extremely sharp. Only take off the thickness of a hair since additional amounts can always be taken off if required. (See Figure 8-B.)

If the new reed is too *hard* (after soaking it and trying it out) place the *plaque* between the two blades of the reed, hold it flat on the index finger of the left hand (See Figure 8-C), and, with the knife in the right hand, scrape *lightly* toward the end of the reed. Thin the reed about one thirty-second of an inch on the tip and a little toward the corners so that when it is held against the light a shading which looks approximately similar to Figure 8-D will be achieved.

Figure 8-E indicates the position of the knife and thumb of the left hand while in the process of shaving the reed. The reed should be held in the left hand with the plaque between the blades as in Figure 8-C. The sharp edge of the knife should then be placed on the reed with the left thumb on the back edge of the knife. The left thumb should be used to control the pressure of the knife to the cane of the reed. This pressure should be very slight.

It should be noted that the strokes should always be *outward*; that is, towards the end of the reed. A small amount of wood should be taken off each time and the cane should remain moist all the while it is being worked on. The reed should be tried continually until the desired strength is achieved. If the reed is too open after soaking and playing, squeeze the very end of the cane together between the thumb and first finger and hold in this position for several minutes. Be certain that the reed is well soaked before attempting this since it will probably crack if it is not.

A great deal of practice on old reeds is strongly recommended before attempting to adjust new ones. Although the basic skills can be taught and numerous books have been written on the subject, the fact remains that *logical experimentation,* or the "trial and error" method, is probably the best way to find out how to work on double reeds.

Oboe reeds will last a long time if they receive proper care. The reed should be put into a reed case after playing. If a reed case is not available, a small cardboard box packed with cotton can be used for this purpose. Glass or celluloid tubes are not satisfactory since the reed cannot get the necessary air to dry properly and will usually begin to rot in a short time. Lipstick is *most harmful* to any reed, single or double.

The oboe reed should be washed at least once a week by using a small pigeon feather. Hold the reed under a water faucet so that the tap water will run into the open end of the tube. Scrub the inside of the reed with the feather. (Brush the feather on soap before scrubbing.) Rinse the reed in clear water.

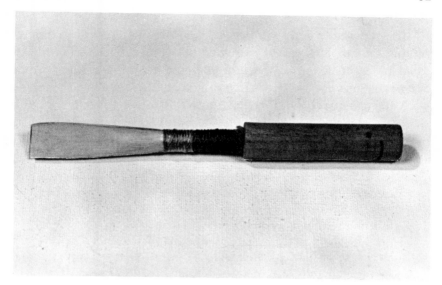

Figure 8–D

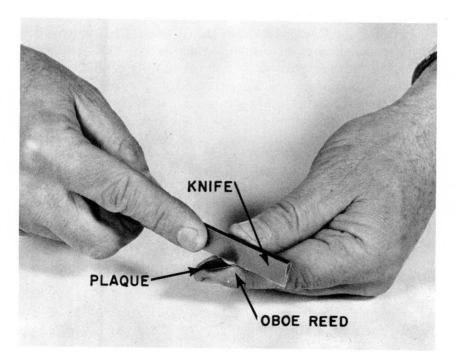

Figure 8–E

Teaching vibrato

It is generally agreed that an unobtrusive, pleasing vibrato should be part and parcel of a good oboe tone. Various specialists tend to differ in terms of when to begin teaching vibrato. Some advocate early instruction while others would commence teaching vibrato at a much later time. Everett Timm's approach to this problem seems to be a logical one:

> When to teach vibrato is a frequent question which cannot be answered in the terms of how long the student has studied. A student is ready to try vibrato as soon as he can control his breath properly and has developed a dependable embouchure and a good basic sound. Some students can do this in a year or less, others may take three years. A student must be able to play in tune and with a pleasing tone before he works on vibrato. Beginning vibrato too early will obscure pitch and tone. Waiting too long may produce a performer who is indifferent to his sound and expression or who may be prejudiced against the use of vibrato.[2]

There are basically three ways to produce vibrato; they are constricting the flow of air in the throat, controlled movement of the jaw, and through the use of the diaphragm. Constricting the flow of air in the throat (or "throat vibrato") is generally considered to be unsatisfactory because it tends to produce a tightening of the throat muscles, and as a result, has a harmful effect on tone quality. Some oboists are able to achieve a pleasing vibrato through the controlled movement of their jaws. The jaw vibrato is probably easier and faster to achieve than that originating in the diaphragm. If it is not carefully controlled, however, the result can be considerably less than satisfactory.

The best method of achieving a vibrato is generally considered to be by employing the diaphragm. This method, if taught and executed properly, will produce an even, well-controlled, and pleasing vibrato. The diaphragm vibrato, in most cases, must be developed over a period of time and should be practiced very slowly at first. A lecture-demonstration by a competent oboist is of great help. The student should be taught to play *loud* and then *soft* at the rate of approximately 76 to 80 metronomic beats per

---

[2]Everett L. Timm, *The Woodwinds* (Boston: Allyn and Bacon, Inc., 1964), p. 14.

minute. Over a period of time this activity should be accelerated to include two *even* pulsations per beat and then increased to four *even* pulsations per beat. The vibrato will eventually become natural and ingrained into the "oboe personality" of the student to the point where it is relegated to his subconscious level.

A selected and annotated list of oboe solo literature for the development of specific individual skills

Arnold, *Sonatina for Oboe and Piano* (Lengnick). This sonatina is a very appealing work in the contemporary English idiom. The moderately advanced oboist should find it to be both interesting and challenging. The piano part is not as difficult as the oboe part. The final movement, when taken up to the proper tempo, requires considerable technical facility of the oboist.

Dittersdorf, *Concerto* (Associated). Most of the classical concertos for the oboe seem to be very demanding. This is probably one of the easier ones and a good one with which to begin the study of classical concertos. The Dittersdorf *Concerto* is good material for the development of the advanced oboist. The accompaniment of this particular work is not excessively demanding.

Guilhard, *First Concertino* (Southern). The *First Concertino* is one of the most popular and widely performed oboe solos on both the secondary and college levels. A considerable amount of technical facility is required of the oboist as well as a flare for the dramatic. Played well, it is a most effective and impressive solo. It is very good material for the study and development of interpretation, coordination of tongue and fingers, and fluent, precise execution of technical passages. The accompaniment is not greatly demanding.

Handel, *Concerto No. 1 in Bb Major* (Boosey & Hawkes). This is another work that should be in the repertory of every oboist. It is not complicated and is generally lyrical. The piano part is idiomatically written and is not excessively demanding. Only a moderately advanced oboist is required. This concerto is an excellent way to introduce the student to the Baroque period of musical literature.

Labate, *Barcarolle* (Carl Fischer). *Barcarolle* is recommended for the young oboist after he has achieved some technical and musical foundation on the instrument. It is a short but pleasant work and is a generally good solo for the student's overall development on the oboe. The accompaniment is technically more difficult than the solo part.

Lebate (arr.), *Oboist's Repertoire Album* (Carl Fischer). Included in this album are twelve arrangements of works by Wagner, Mendelssohn, Handel, Dvorak, and others. The solo oboe parts range from easy to moderately difficult as do the accompaniments. This is good material for the intermediate oboist to study and perform. It can be employed to good effect for the development of interpretation, phrasing, rhythm, and tone quality.

Lefebvre, *Andante & Allegro* (Southern). This is a splendid French art solo for the moderately advanced oboist. The *Andante* section provides much opportunity for developing interpretation and style. A wide range of notation is used in both movements. The *Allegro* section can be used in the development of a smooth, fluent technique. The accompaniment requires a pianist of considerable technical facility as well as musical sensitivity.

Mozart, *Concerto in C Major*, K. 314 (Bossey & Hawkes). Every advanced oboist should eventually have this concerto in his repertory. It demands the precise execution of a considerable amount of sustained rapid technique. This concerto is fine material for the development of both musicianship and technical command of the instrument. The piano reduction requires an advanced performer.

Nielsen, *Romance* and *Humoresque* (Southern). These can be used as individual solos or combined. *Romance* lies well on the instrument and is in an easy key for the oboe. It is good material for the development of interpretation and phrasing. *Humoresque* is technically more demanding but well within the capacity of the moderately advanced player. It can be used for the development of staccato playing and technical facility. Some rhythm problems are present as is a small amount of ornamentation. The accompaniments are on the moderately advanced levels.

Piston, *Suite* (E. C. Schirmer). Published in 1934, the Piston *Suite* is comparatively "old" for a contemporary work. It is comprised of five relatively short movements. There are both much contrast and considerable dissonance in this suite. The oboe part is on the moderately advanced level and the piano part is somewhat less difficult. It is a very good work for introducing the oboist to the contemporary idiom on his instrument.

Saint-Säens, *Sonata for Oboe and Piano*, Opus 166 (Durand, Elkan-Vogel). This sonata should be both challenging and interesting to the advanced oboist. A number of fingering problems are prevalent and a considerable amount of technique is required. Almost all aspects of oboe performance are directly involved; such as, rapid, precise technique, smooth legato playing, rapid staccato, good coordination between tongue and fingers, phrasing, and interpretation. The piano part, however, is not as difficult as the oboe part.

Seventy-Two Oboe Solos (Belwin). Included in this collection are adaptations of works by Mozart, Schubert, Liszt, and Brahms, as well as numerous well-known short pieces. The solo parts range from easy to moderately difficult and the accompaniments are generally easy. This is a good collection for the very young oboist to develop both tone quality and phrasing. It also affords him the opportunity to become accustomed to performing solo literature with the piano.

Schumann, *Three Romances* (G. Schirmer). These comprise sonata-style oboe literature at its best. *Three Romances* is excellent for the development of musical phrasing, style, and interpretation. Technically, the solo parts are not difficult. A great deal of endurance, however, is required in the performance of these solos. The piano parts should not prove to be exceedingly difficult for the pianist of some experience. They are idiomatically written for this instrument.

Warren, *Meditation* (Ludwig). A good solo for the young oboist, *Meditation* does not burden the performer with great technical demands. It is often used as one of the oboist's first solos in the study and development of tone quality, intonation, and phrasing. The accompaniment is easy.

Weinberger, *Sonatine* (Carl Fischer). *Sonatine* is recommended for the young oboist of any age. Technically, the solo part is not demanding and gives the oboist opportunity to concentrate on tone quality, intonation, and phrasing. Musically, it should also serve to introduce him to the sonata as a composition. The accompaniment is easy.

Selected bibliography

Bate, Philip, *The Oboe.* New York: Philosophical Library, 1956.

Fitch, William D. "Transfer to Oboe," *The Instrumentalist*, vol. 17, December, 1962, p. 57.

Gassman, Bert, "The Oboist and the Reed," *Woodwind World*, vol. 4, April, 1963, p. 9.

Groth, Earl, "Technical Problems of the Oboe in the Band," (Part I), *The Instrumentalist*, vol. 21, January, 1967, p. 38.

Groth, Earl, "Technical Problems of the Oboe in the Band," (Part II), *The Instrumentalist*, vol. 21, February, 1967, p. 46.

Groth, Earl, "Technical Problems of the Oboe in the Band," (Part III), *The Instrumentalist*, vol. 21, May, 1967, p. 54.

Groth, Earl, "Technical Problems of the Oboe in the Band," (Part IV), *The Instrumentalist*, vol. 21, June, 1967, p. 44.

Hussey, George A., "Making the Long Lay Oboe Reed," *The Instrumentalist*, vol. 20, September, 1965, p. 54.

Lehman, Paul R., *Teacher's Guide to the Oboe*. Elkhart, Indiana: H.& A. Selmer, Inc., 1965.

Mayer, R., & T. Rohner, *Oboe Reeds: How to Make and Adjust Them*. Evanston, Illinois: The Instrumentalist Co., 1953.

Moore, E. C., *The Oboe Book*. Kenosha, Wisconsin: G. Leblanc Co., 1957.

Organ, Robert J., *The Oboe, Performance—Teaching*. Denver, Colorado: Rebo Publishing Co., 1954.

Rothwell, Evelyn, *Oboe Technique*. New York: Oxford University Press. 1962.

Russell, Myron E., *Oboe Reed Making and Problems of the Oboe Player*. Stamford, Connecticut: Jack Spratt Co., 1963.

Soderstrom, Jim, "Working With Oboe Reeds—Some Special Tips for Music Teachers," *Woodwind World*, vol. 6, September, 1966, p. 11.

Spratt, Jack, *How to Make Double Reeds*. Stamford, Connecticut: Jack Spratt Co., 1950.

Sprenkle, Robert, "Preparation or Anticipation," *Woodwind World*, vol. 3, December, 1959, p. 10.

Sprenkle, Robert & Ledet, David, *The Art of Oboe Playing*. Evanston, Illinois: Summy-Birchard Co., 1961.

Timm, Everett L., *The Woodwinds*. Boston: Allyn Bacon Co., 1964.

CHAPTER 9

The Flute

The flute is undoubtedly the most ancient of all the woodwind instruments. Legend has passed down the belief that the sound produced by the whistling wind across hollow river reeds first gave man the idea of constructing this instrument. The present day flute was developed by the professional flutist, Theobald Böehm (1794–1881). Due to modern manufacturing research and techniques, first-line flutes are normally constructed very well in tune. Versatile as both a solo and ensemble instrument, the flute section constitutes a very important part of the modern concert band. Some relatively basic aspects of flute pedagogy and performance are included since it is felt that instrumental instructors might find value in referring to them.

Selecting instructional materials

While beginning material available to the flutist is rather limited, moderately advanced and advanced literature is quite abundant. Beginning methods are included here only as a possible reference source for the interested instructor.

Beginning Methods

Rubank Elementary Method .... Peterson-Rubank
Universal Fundamental Method .... Melnik-Universal
A Tune a Day for Flute (in two volumes) .... Herfurth-Stuart,
                                                              Boston Music Co.
Eck Method for Flute, Book I .... Eck-Belwin

Intermediate Methods

Eck Method for Flute, Book II .... Eck-Belwin
Rubank Intermediate Method .... Skornicka-Petersen, Rubank
Flute Method (in two volumes) .... Rex Elton Fair-Cole
Rubank Advanced Method (in two volumes) .... Voxman-Rubank

Medium Advanced Methods

Melodious & Progressive Studies,
     Volume I .... Cavally-Southern Music Co.
Modern Pares for Flute .... Pares, Whistler-Rubank
24 Short Melodious Studies with Variations .... Moyse-Belwin

Advanced Methods

Melodious and Progressive Studies,
     Volumes II and III .... Cavally-Southern Music Co.
Modern Flutist .... Andraud-Southern Music Co.
Selected Studies for the Flute .... Voxman-Rubank
18 Studies for the Flute .... Berbiguier-G. Schirmer
12 Daily Exercises for Development of
     Tone and Technique .... Wummer-Belwin
26 Selected Studies for Flute .... Altes-G. Schirmer
24 Etudes, Opus 15 .... Andersen-Southern Music Co.
24 Progressive Studies, Opus 33 .... Andersen-Southern Music Co.

Choosing flute, student adaptability, flute recordings, and care of the flute

A better value is usually obtained by purchasing a medium grade instrument for the flute student rather than the lowest priced instrument on the market. The medium grade instrument will, in most cases, perform better, wear better, last longer, and have greater resale or trade-in value. The difference in cost between the lowest priced instrument and the medium grade flute is usually not excessive. Basically, there are two model Böehm flutes, the *closed hole* and the *open hole* or *French-Model* flute.

Most professional flutists and teachers tend to prefer the open hole flute and all of the leading flute manufacturing firms produce and market this instrument. The open hole flute appears to be used more and more by intermediate and advanced flute students as well as by professional flutists. Many music educators, however, still prefer the closed hole instrument for beginning students. The help of a competent flutist in selecting an instrument is of great value.

The flute student, like any other music student, must possess a certain degree of musical sensitivity and talent. He should have a good sense of pitch, rhythm, and a strong desire to play the instrument. In general, a good indication of talent for the flute is the student's ability to produce tones on the head joint of the instrument after some instruction showing how to go about doing this. Students with heavy, thick lips will probably experience considerable difficulty in getting a good sound on the flute. Timm lists three handicaps to producing a tone on this instrument:

1. Too much "cupid's bow" in the upper lip. The center of the upper lip may drop so low that instead of lifting to form an opening for the air stream, it divides the air into two streams.

2. "Buck" or protruding upper front teeth may make it impossible to direct the air stream where it should go. A lower jaw which protrudes too far can also misdirect the air stream.

3. Lips which are deeply wrinkled, rough, frequently very chapped, or insensitive may make flute and piccolo playing impossible or highly impractical.[1]

The following recordings can be used to demonstrate the flute:

"The Instruments of the Orchestra (with narrator and performed by first desk men of the Vienna State Opera Orchestra), Vanguard records #VRS-1017 and VRS-1018.

"Poem for Flute and Orchestra" by Griffes, William Kincaid, Flutist, Columbia #ML 4629.

"Flute Contest Music," Charles DeLaney, Flutist, Selmer records No. 2900 and No. 2942.

---

[1]Everett L. Timm, *The Woodwinds* (Boston: Allyn and Bacon, Inc., 1964), p. 35.

"Concerto for Flute and Orchestra" by Jacques Ibert, Julius Baker, Flutist, Oxford #OR 104.

"Flutists' Showcase" (solos, duets, trios, and quartets) recorded by Blaisdell, Kortkamp, Moskovitz, Panitz, Pellerite, and Wilkins. Golden Crest Record #CR 4020.

"James Pellerite Flute Recital," James Pellerite, flutist, Ashley Miller, Pianist. Golden Crest Record #RE-7010.

"Flute Solos," Sarah Baird Fouse, flutist, Cecilia Ewing, Pianist. Coronet Program LP #1245.

Like any other musical instrument, the flute requires good care if it is expected to function well. The instrument should be swabbed out thoroughly after each time it is played. Any clean, absorbent cloth will make a good swab. The outside of the flute should be carefully wiped off with this cloth before returning the instrument to its case. To maintain good key action apply a very small amount of light-weight key oil to every point of friction between key hinges and posts as well as at points where the key hinges meet. This should be done about every two or three months depending on the season of the year; that is, more frequently in the warm, humid months and less frequently in the winter months. Never use silver polish or a treated cleaning cloth on the flute. Water can be removed from pads and/or tone holes by using cigarette paper. The cork in the head joint of the flute should only be adjusted by a skilled woodwind repair specialist. Indeed, some instrumental teachers have gone to the extreme of having it soldered fast so that it cannot be moved. The reason for not tampering with this cork is that it has been carefully adjusted to control the fundamental intonation of the instrument. Finally, the student must exercise great care in order not to squeeze the rods when assembling the flute. Complete and detailed instructions regarding the care of the flute are available, usually at little or no cost, from every flute manufacturing firm. Students and teachers of this instrument should be thoroughly acquainted with them.

Teaching flute playing

The Embouchure and the Sound. One of the greatest problems of the flutist is that of getting a good, clear sound on the instrument. The flute is unique in that its tone is produced by a vibrating air column. This is most easily demonstrated by blowing across the open end of a bottle. The following two steps are recommended to achieve a basic embouchure formation:

1. The hole formed by the lips must not be as wide as the air hole in the instrument.
2. The lips should be free from wrinkles.

The embouchure can then be formed by placing the lips directly on top of each other. The lips should be stretched very slightly toward the corners of the mouth to make a smooth surface. Both upper and lower lips should be as even as possible.

A small hole should be opened in the center of the lips and the head joint of the flute should be placed on the chin so that about a third of the hole is covered by the lower lip and two-thirds should remain open. The sound which should result will be an open C#.

It is recommended that the beginning flute player spend much time in experimenting with blowing on the *mouthpipe alone* and striving for a clear, unimpeded sound. Most students have a tendency to use far more air than is actually needed. There is virtually no resistance to the breath stream if the player wants to use a great deal of air in his efforts to play the flute. The amount of breath expended should be extremely economical and the player should continually check the size of the hole in his lips. A good deal of practice in front of a mirror is useful. (See Figure 9-A.)

The position of the player's head should be erect and facing forward. The flute may be permitted to point slightly toward the floor. This will tend to make the arms more comfortable. The knuckle joint of the index finger (of the left hand) should be flush to the instrument and the left thumb should never be bent. The right thumb should be placed on the bottom side of the flute and used to hold it in place. (See Figure 9-B.)

The flute student should be taught to start all tones with his tongue and to tongue many notes with one steady column of air. The air should proceed through an elliptical hole located at approximately the center of the player's mouth. The tip of the tongue should be placed behind the upper teeth at approximately the place where teeth and gums meet. This is essentially the same position of the tongue when pronouncing the word "tongue." The

Figure 9–A   Flute Embouchure Position

Figure 9–B   Flute Embouchure and Hand Position

tongue is then pulled down with a minimum of motion, employing the syllable TU. Caution is recommended at this point to
avoid any change in the embouchure. The movement of the
tongue should always be rapid and should take place simultaneously with the projection of breath into the flute. After the marcato attack (TU) is controlled the legato should be taught by sub-
stituting the syllable DU.

Teaching Multiple Tonguing. After the flutist has acquired considerable technical facility and has mastered single tonguing on
his instrument, he is ready to begin work on the multiple tonguing
techniques. Into this group fall double tonguing, triple tonguing,
and flutter tonguing. The multiple tonguings are employed only
where they are required; such as, in rapid repetitions of one note
or in excessively fast passages. The single tongue should be used
if possible. The flute is unique in the use of multiple tonguings
since the other woodwinds do not generally use them.

Double tonguing must be confined to passages where notes are
grouped in two's. Much advanced flute étude material deals with
developing this facet of flute performance. It can be achieved by
pronouncing the syllables TU-KU. (See Figure 9-C.)

TU KU TU KU   TU KU TU KU   TU KU TU KU

Figure 9–C

On the first syllable (TU) the tongue is in the identical position
as it is for single tonguing. The second syllable (KU) is achieved
by the tongue touching the palate, thus stopping the flow of air.
Much slow practice is required in the development of a good
double tonguing technique. Clearly, a student who has a naturally
slow single tongue will probably need to develop and rely upon
double tonguing more than one who has a naturally rapid single
tongue. It should be pointed out that it is quite possible to perfect
double tonguing on the flute to the point where it is very difficult
to distinguish it from single tonguing.

Triple tonguing is employed where notes are grouped in threes
or where one note needs to be tongued very rapidly in the form

of triplets. As can be readily seen by Figure 9-D, it is closely related to double tonguing.

Figure 9–D

It is perhaps a common problem with nearly all wind instrumentalists that tone quality tends to deteriorate during tongued passages. The student needs to guard against this. The quality of tone also seems to decline when excessive amounts of practice time are spent on tonguing exercises of one sort or another. A rapid tongue (either single or multiple) should never be developed at the expense of the student's tone quality. Actually, there would seem to be no logical reason why both tone and tonguing cannot be developed simultaneously.

Flutter Tonguing on the Flute. Flutter tonguing is actually more of a special effect than an articulation per se. It was probably first employed by Richard Strauss and is used, from time to time, in contemporary musical literature. For this special effect the tongue should be rolled quite rapidly against the roof of the player's mouth, such as in rolling the letter "r."

Both good tone quality and good intonation are very much related to proper breathing. Deep diaphragmatic breathing is, of course, very important in the performance on any wind instrument. This is perhaps more so on the flute. Too many wind instrument players practice the habit of shallow "chest" breathing instead of breathing deeply by employing the diaphragm. Correct breathing should be taught from the onset of the student's instruction. Proper breath support, resulting from deep diaphragmatic breathing, contributes vitally to the following important aspects of flute performance: tone production, accurate intonation, musical phrasing, and control of dynamics. The most significant portion of the breath is that which *backs up* the tone in the form of support. Vibrato too would seem to be directly related to good breath control. Since vibrato might be construed to be an addition to the tone it would seem logical to teach tone quality and breath support first. After these have been acquired vibrato should be introduced. The diaphragm vibrato probably produces the best results. (See Chapter 8, "The Oboe.") Among the chief reasons for using this type of vibrato are that it requires no change in embouchure and that it can be well controlled throughout the entire range of the instrument.

A selected and annotated list of flute solo literature for the development of specific individual skills

Andersen-Cavally, *The Mill* (Southern). Probably the chief values of this solo are for the development of a fluent and precise technique and adequate breath control to support this technique. Another principal point for the student to concentrate on during the study and performance of *The Mill* is the maintenance of good tone quality throughout the solo. It is a common pitfall for the student to concentrate so much on the technical aspect of instrumental performance that he forgets the importance of maintaining good tone quality. Although the accompaniment has several difficult areas it is not generally demanding.

J. S. Bach, *Suite in B Minor* (Cundy-Bettoney). Every moderately advanced and advanced flute student should study and perform the Bach suites and sonatas for this instrument. A moderately advanced flutist is required for this particular suite which was originally scored for flute and strings. This fine baroque work is good for the development of technical facility, phrasing, breath support, and overall musicianship on the flute. The piano part requires a moderately advanced performer.

Bournonville, *Danse Pour Katia* (Edition Costallat). This is a fine solo (perhaps a "first" solo) for the young flutist. It is particularly good for achieving and projecting tone quality in the flute's low register, the development of interpretation and phrasing, and working toward a good staccato on the flute. The accompaniment is not difficult.

Chaminade, *Concertino* (Associated). *Concertino* is another virtual "must" for the advanced flute student to study and perform. It is good for the development of nearly all aspects of musical performance through the flute medium, including technique, phrasing, breath support, interpretation, tone quality, and tonguing. An advanced pianist is also required.

Doppler-Cavally, *Berceuse* (Southern). This solo should afford the intermediate flute student a number of opportunities for technical and musical development on his instrument. First, he will find himself playing in a key (four sharps) somewhat foreign to many secondary school flute students. *Berceuse* is also a good solo for extending the student's high register and developing breath control. The accompaniment is not as difficult as the solo part.

Griffes, *Poem* (Carl Fischer). *Poem* is a favorite virtuoso piece with the advanced flutist. There are beautiful lyrical sections requiring much breath support and projection of tone. Considerable technique is called for in the mid-section, including the use of double tonguing. The solo concludes with another slow lyrical section. Command of both the low and high registers is essential in this solo. The accompaniment is also on the advanced level.

Handel, *Sonata #1 for Flute and Piano* (Cundy-Bettoney). Every flute student should be acquainted with the Handel flute sonatas. *Sonata #1* should provide the intermediate student with a good introduction to this fine baroque flute literature. No problem of wide range is involved. This sonata will, however, be good for the development of accuracy in counting, phrasing, breath support, and technical facility. The piano part is generally not difficult.

Hanson, *Serenade* (Carl Fischer). *Serenade* is fine solo material for the moderately advanced to advanced flute student. It is written in the modern idiom and presents a number of challenges to the flutist including technical precision, rhythmic accuracy, breath control, rubato playing, and various articulation problems. The piano reduction requires a pianist of considerable technical skill and musical sensitivity.

Hindemith, *Sonata for Flute and Piano* (Associated). The Hindemith *Sonata for Flute* is rather widely performed by ambitious high school flute students. Moderately advanced flute and piano students should be able to profit from the study and performance of this interesting and appealing sonata.

Kennan, *Night Soliloquy* (Carl Fischer). Nearly every advanced flute student eventually studies this excellent contemporary American solo. Both piano and flute parts require performers of considerable technical development and musical sensitivity. It is an especially good solo for the study and development of rhythm.

Kinyon (arr.), *Breeze-Easy Recital Pieces* (Witmark). This is a very good collection for the young flutist to study and perform after he has achieved a basic foundation on his instrument. Technically, the material used in this collection is not demanding, and the student should have ample time to concentrate on such aspects of performance as tone production, breath support, intonation, and phrasing. The accompaniments are generally easy.

Massenet-Cavally, *Melodie-Elegie* (Southern). Breath control, tone production, phrasing, rhythm, and dynamic control are stressed in this comparatively brief solo. The technical and musical requirements lie well within the capacity of the first or second year flute student. The accompaniment is also on the easy level.

Mozart, *Concerto No. 1 in G Major* K. 313 (Boosey & Hawkes). This concerto is rightly studied and performed by most serious students of the flute. As is the case with so many other Mozart wind concerts, the flute concerto is regrettably performed too frequently by students who do not have the necessary musical maturity to perform such a work. Like the other Mozart wind concertos, the flute concerto is not an easy work to do well. It requires an advanced student of considerable musical sensitivity, as well as technical facility, and is an excellent piece for the development of all aspects of flute performance. The piano reduction, while not exceedingly difficult, requires a sensitive advanced performer on this instrument.

Mozart-Moyse, *Three Sonatas for Flute and Piano* (G. Schirmer). These recently published sonatas have been adapted from the Flute Quartets of Mozart (K. 285, 285b, and 298) by the celebrated flutist, Louis Moyse. They should provide a genuine musical challenge to the intermediate or moderately advanced flute student in terms of developing good coordination between tongue and fingers, rhythm, interpretation, execution of various ornamental figures, and extension of range. The piano adaptations should not be forbiddingly difficult for the moderately advanced pianist.

Piston, *Sonata for Flute and Piano* (Associated). This is one of the finest contemporary American works for the flute. Technically, the final movement will demand much even of the advanced player. It is a good work for both the musical and technical development of the advanced flutist. The piano part also requires an advanced performer.

Voxman (edited), *Concert and Contest Collection for Flute* (Rubank). Included in this collection are works by Handel, Donjon, J. S. Bach, Joachim Andersen and others. The technical and musical difficulty of these solos places them on the intermediate to moderately difficult levels. They can be used to advantage in the development of most aspects of musicianship on the flute, including the high register, rhythm, tone production, phrasing, staccato and legato playing, and technical facility. The accompaniments are not greatly demanding.

Selected bibliography

Baker, Julius, "Flute Playing in the United States," *Woodwind World*, vol. 3, December, 1959, p. 7.

Böehm, Theobold, *The Flute and Flute Playing* translated by D. C. Miller. London: Rudall, Corte and Co., 1922. (available from McGinnis & Marx, New York City.)

Chapman, F. B., *Flute Technique*. London: Oxford University Press, 1958.

Collis, James, "The First Lady of the Flute," *Woodwind World*, vol. 3, September, 1959, p. 8.

LeJeune, Harriet Peacock, *A Flutist's Manual*. Evanston, Illinois: Summy-Birchard Co., 1964.

Macdonald, Donald, "Your Flutes Don't Have to Play Out of Tune," *The Instrumentalist*, vol. 19, April, 1965, p. 94.

Maher, James, "Mrs. Dwyer's Left-Handed Flute," *Woodwind World*, vol. 3, February, 1960, p. 6.

Moore, E. C., *The Flute and Its Daily Routine*. Kenosha, Wisconsin: Leblanc Publications Inc., 1962.

Moskovitz, Harry, "Alto Flute," *Woodwind World*, vol. 6, September, 1965, p. 4.

Moskovitz, Harry, "The Versatile E Flat Soprano Flute," *Woodwind World*, vol. 5, February, 1964, p. 4.

Pellerite, James, "The French-Model Flute: A Re-Appraisal," *The Instrumentalist*, vol. 28, December, 1963, p. 62.

Pellerite, James, *A Handbook of Literature for the Flute*. Bloomington, Indiana: Zalo Publications, 1963.

Pellerite, James, *A Modern Guide to Fingerings for the Flute*. Bloomington, Indiana: Zalo Publications, 1964.

Rohner, Traugott, "Expanding the Flute Family," *The Instrumentalist*, vol. 27, June, 1963, p. 54.

Taylor, Laurence, "Difficulty with Upper Notes," *The Instrumentalist*, vol. 28, May, 1964, p. 74.

Timm, Everett L., *The Woodwinds*. Boston, Mass.: Allyn and Bacon, Inc., 1964.

Waln, Ronald L., "The Beginning Flutist," *The Instrumentalist*, vol. 19, October, 1964, p. 65.

Westphal, Frederick W., *Guide to Teaching Woodwinds*. Dubuque, Iowa: Wm. C. Brown Company, 1962.

CHAPTER 10

The Saxophone

The saxophone family, including the bass and soprano saxophones, has a pitch range which approximates that of the clarinet family. Since its invention by Adolph Sax in 1846, the saxophone has received a wider acceptance in Europe, particularly in France, than in the United States. It should be pointed out, however, that the saxophone is growing in popularity and it is now possible to "major" in the saxophone in the majority of American schools of music. A number of the larger universities now have faculty members who are specialists in the areas of saxophone performance and pedagogy. Within the setting of the modern concert band a fine saxophone section is a most valuable asset. In addition a number of composers have included this instrument in their works for symphony orchestra.

Selecting instructional materials

The amount of intermediate and advanced instructional materials written especially for the saxophone is somewhat limited. Since the saxophone and oboe have identical playing ranges, it is recommended that oboe instructional materials be used (see Chapter 8).

Beginning Methods

Universal Fundamental Method .... Universal
Rubank Elementary Method .... Rubank
Rubank Elementary Method .... Rubank
Adventures in Saxophone Playing (Bodegraven)
  (Volume I) .... Staff Music Pub. Co.

Intermediate Methods

Belwin Method, Book II (Cailliet) .... Belwin
Universal Follow-Up Method .... Universal
Rubank Intermediate Method .... Rubank
Adventures in Saxophone Playing (Bodegraven)
  (Volume II) .... Staff Music Pub. Co.

Advanced Methods and Supplementary Studies

Selected Studies for Saxophone (Voxman) .... Rubank
Technical Studies (Tustin) .... Peer International
Virtuoso Studies (Traxler-Lazarus) .... Belwin
158 Exercises (Rascher) .... Wilhelm Hansen
30 Caprices (Cavallini-Iasilli) .... Carl Fischer
48 Studies for Oboe or Saxophone .... Southern
The Saxophonist's Workbook (Teal) .... U. of Michigan Music Press
Studies in High Harmonics (Nash) .... Leeds
Top Tones for the Saxophone (Rascher) .... Carl Fischer

Choosing a saxophone, student adaptability, saxophone recordings, and care of the saxophone

With regard to choosing a saxophone (or any other instrument), a strong case can be made for purchasing a *medium-priced* instrument rather than the *least expensive* instrument on the market. The difference in cost between these two grades is normally not exceedingly great, whereas there is usually a considerable difference in the quality of the instruments. Dollar-for-dollar the medium-priced instrument is usually the best buy. It should also be remembered that, in many cases, the first instrument purchased for a student remains with him throughout his secondary school days and even longer. When buying a saxophone it is recommended that the student consult his instrumental music teacher and/or a professional performer on the saxophone. The specialist should check the instrument for good intonation, ease of blowing, mechanical adjustment, and tone quality.

A set standard of specific physical requirements for the saxophone student cannot be relied upon. Actually, if the student is physically large enough to hold the instrument and has normal lips, teeth, and chin, he can probably play the saxophone. Many regard this instrument as the easiest standard beginning instrument. In most cases the best beginning saxophone is the alto. Success on the saxophone, of course, also presupposes a good general intelligence, musical aptitude, a strong desire to play the instrument, and the ability to develop fruitful practice habits.

The following recordings are suggested for use in teaching the saxophone:

"Saxophone Solos," Eugene Rousseau, Saxophonist. Coronet Program LP #1292.

"Contest and Concert Solos for the Saxophone," Harley Rex, Saxophonist. Austin Custom Record #6601.

"Marcel Mule Saxophone Recital," Available from Selmer, Inc.

"American Music for Saxophone," Donald Sinta, Saxophonist. Mark Records Recital Series.

"A Classical Recital on the Saxophone," Sigurd Rascher, Saxophonist. Concert Hall Society #1156.

"Contest Music for Saxophone," Fred Hemke, Saxophonist. Selmer record #4150.

Although the saxophone is normally a well-constructed, sturdy instrument the following points should be observed relative to its care. Books and/or music should never be carried in the saxophone case since this will often bend keys and otherwise damage the instrument. The cork on the mouthpipe should be greased and the bore cleaned from time to time. The neckpipe should be shaken after playing and swabbed out frequently. The instrument should be checked and adjusted once a year by a professional woodwind repairman. The student should clean and oil the saxophone completely three or more times during the year and carefully dust around the instrument with a small paint brush frequently. A good quality instrument which is given adequate care can be used for long periods of time with only minor repairs and adjustments. Detailed instructions for the care of the saxophone are available from any manufacturer.

Teaching saxophone playing

The student should sit or stand erect. The shoulders should be back with both feet on the floor. This position should not be rigid or stiff, but relaxed and poised. The neck strap should be adjusted to the point where the head does not have to be either raised or lowered. The hands should be relaxed at all times.

Saxophone Embouchure. The recommended embouchure for the saxophone is similar to that used for the clarinet; that is, approximately one-half of the *red* of the lower lip should rest on the mouthpiece about one-half inch from the tip. The mouthpiece should be held securely between the upper and lower lips but without excessive pressure. There should be no "biting" on the mouthpiece and reed and the cheeks should not be puffed out. The throat should be open at all times. (See Figures 10-A and 10-B.)

The tip of the tongue should touch the tip of the reed a little below the edge. Only the tongue should move (not the chin and jaw). The tone should be started by the tongue hitting the reed and not by the breath. The tone should be stopped by the breath and not by the tongue; that is, the tone should stop when the breath stops.

Correct Saxophone Tone. In general, the student should be encouraged to strive for a mellow, rich, refined, singing tone quality. High quality equipment (saxophone, mouthpiece, ligature, and reed) will be a great aid, but perhaps of even greater importance is the need for the student to have a good *concept* of what a musical sound on the saxophone should be. This can be attained by listening to fine saxophone artists perform, either in person or on recording. A good way to study one's own tone quality is to develop the habit of careful listening during the playing of long tones and slow études. A first-line tape recorder can be of invaluable assistance here, not only for the study of tone quality alone, but for studying one's total musical performance on the saxophone. Clearly, the student should constantly study his tone quality and strive to improve it. By its very nature this is a slow process and the student should not expect to attain miraculous results overnight.

The tone should be supported from the diaphragm at all times. The shrill, harsh, cutting sound frequently associated with dance and jazz band saxophonists should be avoided. The student should look upon the improvement of tone quality as a lifetime study.

Figure 10–A   Saxophone in Playing Position, Front View

Figure 10–B   Saxophone in Playing Position, Side View

Breaking in and adjusting single reeds

Since single reed players comprise a large segment of our present day bands it would seem important that they have a workable approach to breaking in and adjusting their reeds. Regrettably, few school music students apparently have adequate knowledge concerning this important aspect of their playing. This is evidenced, in part at least, by the following typical examples:

1. The *laissez faire* approach; that is, a reed is put on the mouthpiece and if it does not function satisfactorily it is immediately discarded and the same procedure repeated.
2. The reed is clipped with a scissors and scraped with a knife or razor blade.
3. One reasonably playable reed is used sometimes for several months or until it completely ceases to function.
4. The habit of using reeds that are coated with lipstick or food particles.

In considering the problem of working with single reeds the following preliminary remarks should be observed:

1. The side edges of the reed should not be squeezed against the mouthpiece by the ligature. Rather, the pressure of the ligature should be in the center of the reed.
2. The ligature should be approximately one-quarter of an inch below the upper line drawn on most mouthpieces.
3. The upper screw of the ligature should *not* be tightened —tighten only the lower screw.
4. The reed should be kept clean at all times. It should be noted that lipstick is especially harmful to any reed, single or double.

The reed problems of most single reed instrument players are greatly aggravated by not observing the above points.

Selection of Reeds. The first step in preparing new reeds is to select four or five reeds from the box. At this stage it does not matter a great deal if the reed is too soft or too strong, the important point being that it must vibrate freely. Next, wet all the reeds completely, place them on a glass, and massage the vamps thoroughly with the ball of the thumb. The reeds should then be tried and, if too soft, clipped to the desired strength with a high quality reed trimmer specifically designed for the particular reed to be trimmed. (For example, when trimming alto saxophone reeds use an alto saxophone reed trimmer and not an alto clarinet reed trimmer.) If some reeds are too strong do not scrape them at this time because they may become softer after playing. Both clipping and scraping should be approached with caution since it is very easy to ruin a fine reed by just a little too much of either. The reeds should then be left alone for some time in order to dry out thoroughly.

The next time the reeds are tried they should be played for no more than five minutes since good, live cane loses its resilience rapidly in the early stages of the breaking-in period. Let the reeds dry out again for about two hours and try them once more. Clip those that are too soft, and those that are too hard can be softened by lightly scraping the lower right edge with Dutch-rush. Leave the reeds for a day and again play them for a few minutes each, clipping and scraping them as needed.

By this time marked differences in the playing qualities of the reeds will become apparent. The tendency to choose the best reed and neglect the others should be avoided since the life of the reeds will be greatly extended if they are broken in together and used in rotation; that is, rotated every three or four days. The routine of playing, clipping, and scraping the reeds should be continued for several more days in order to achieve the proper resistance and the best results. (See Figure 10-C.)

Scraping the Reed. Two important points that remain to be made are: (1) Do not use a knife or razor blade to scrape the reed and (2) do not scrape a reed in the center. Scraping a reed with a knife or razor blade makes ridges in the reed which are serious defects. Dutch-rush is the best mild abrasive to use. The reason one should not scrape the center of the reed is that the reed vibrates very little there, where its principal function is to offer resistance to the lip. The amplitude of a reed's vibration increases away from the center zone and is at its maximum at the tips and sides of the reed. As stated previously, if the reed is too hard, scrape the lower right edge.

It should also be mentioned that a reed too soft on the left side will not vibrate well, whereas the reverse will not affect its performance. This is caused by the right hand's twisting the instru-

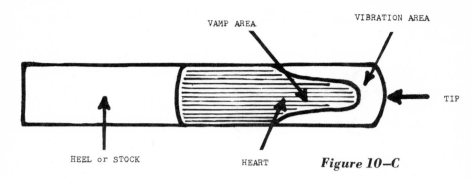

Figure 10—C

ment slightly, resulting in the left side of the reed being pressed harder against the lip. This situation probably affects clarinet players more than it does saxophone players since the latter instrument is largely supported by a neck strap. Consequently, the reed must have more resistance at this point to offset the extra pressure.

Selecting and breaking in reeds requires great patience as well as a knowledge of the fundamental principles. By understanding the basic factors involved, players can save themselves much frus-ration and secure a significantly greater proportion of playable reeds.

Teaching vibrato

Vibrato is, of course, widely used and accepted on the saxophone. Here again three basic approaches are used: (1) the diaphragm vibrato, (2) the throat vibrato, and (3) the lip or jaw vibrato. On the saxophone the *lip* or *jaw* method of producing vibrato is the most widely accepted. The student should not attempt to produce a vibrato until he is able to achieve a pleasing, basic tone on his instrument. The jaw vibrato is comparably easy to develop. Firstly, the jaw must be relaxed. The *slight* motion of the jaw essential in the production of the vibrato must not alter or affect the normal embouchure formation. This slight jaw motion must be accomplished in a controlled rhythm. Practice with a metronome is often helpful at this point. Clearly, the use of a wide vibrato should be avoided. Vibrato should always be used with good taste and discretion. The actual function of vibrato should be to enhance a basically good saxophone sound. It should never be used in an attempt to hide poor intonation or a fundamentally poor tone quality.

A selected and annotated list of saxophone solo literature[1] for the development of specific individual skills

Bennett, *Saxophone Royale* (Southern). *Saxophone Royale* features the development of rubato and the execution of cadenza-style playing. A considerable amount of coordination between tongue and fingers is also required and the final (*allegro*) section demands smooth, accurate technical facility. The accompaniment is generally not difficult and the solo part is on the moderately difficult level. A band accompaniment is also available for this solo.

Benson, *Aeolion Song* (Boosey & Hawkes). This is a comparatively brief solo in the modern idiom. It lies well within the range of the instrument and is especially appropriate for the development of tone quality, breath control, phrasing, and interpretation. The solo part is on the moderately easy level and its accompaniment is not difficult.

Bonneau, *Suite* (Leduc). This is a deservedly popular suite with the moderately advanced saxophonist. Its four movements are entitled *Improvisation, Danse des demons, Plainte*, and *Espieglerie*. The first movement poses some problems in terms of ensemble between the saxophone and piano. The third movement is particularly appropriate for the development of tone quality. The second movement is probably the most difficult for the pianist, and an advanced performer on this instrument is recommended for the study and performance of this suite.

Bournonville-Gee, *Danse pour Katia* (Southern). *Danse pour Katia* is an effective, although rather brief, solo on the moderately easy level. In it the saxophone student will find opportunity for the development of legato and staccato playing, the extension of his range, and coordination between tongue and fingers. The accompaniment is also on the moderately easy level.

---

[1] Foreign publications may be obtained from the following sources:

McGinnis and Marx
148 West 67th Street
New York, New York 10023

M. Baron
Box 149
Oyster Bay, Long Island, New York 11771

Elkan-Vogel Company
1712 Sansom Street
Philadelphia, Pennsylvania 19103

Bedford Hills Music Importers
Box 277
Bedford Hills, New York 10507

Bozza, *Caprice* (Leduc). *Caprice* is an especially fine display piece for the advanced saxophonist. It requires high level development in all aspects of saxophone performance, including an advanced technical command of the instrument as well as a high degree of musical sensitivity. An advanced pianist is also required.

Contemporary French Recital Pieces (International). These pieces are published in two volumes and are generally short in duration. They are witty, clever, and quite interesting to study and perform. A fairly advanced pianist is required. The saxophone parts are, for the most part, on the moderately advanced level.

Creston, *Sonata for Saxophone and Piano* (Shawnee). Nearly every advanced saxophonist studies this fine contemporary sonata. The lyrical second movement is especially appropriate for the display of tone quality and phrasing. The final movement is probably the most difficult in terms of technical facility and ensemble between the two instruments. An advanced pianist is required for the study and performance of this work.

Creston, *Suite* (Shawnee). The movements of this suite are entitled *scherzoso, pastorale,* and *toccata.* The first and third movements involve considerable technical command of the saxophone including a light and rapid staccato. The middle movement (with mute) stresses tone quality, phrasing, and breath control. Advanced performers on both instruments are required.

Gurewich, *Fantasy in F Minor* (Ricordi). *Fantasy in F Minor* is an effective display piece for the moderately advanced saxophone student. The opening section stresses cadenza-style playing, the mid-section accuracy of rhythm, tone quality, and phrasing, and the concluding section clean, precise technical facility. It is also a good solo for the extension of the student's range on the saxophone. The accompaniment is not difficult.

Händel-Rascher, *Sonata No. 3* (Chappell). This is a deservedly popular and much performed arrangement. The first movement (*adagio*) should aid in the development of tone quality and breath support, the second movement (*allegro*) stresses technical facility and coordination between tongue and fingers, the third movement (*largo*) smooth legato playing and phrasing, and the fourth movement (*allegro*) fluent and precise technique. Both saxophone and piano parts are on the moderately difficult level.

Heiden, *Sonata for Saxophone and Piano* (Schott). This is a challenging work for the advanced saxophonist and pianist that poses a number of problems in terms of ensemble between the two instruments.

Its overall style is somewhat reminiscent of Hindemith. This sonata is good for the development of all aspects of musical performance through the saxophone medium. Both parts require the performers to have considerable technical facility and musical maturity.

Ibert, *Concertino da Camera* (Leduc). This work should be in the repertory of every advanced saxophonist. It is one of the best contemporary works for the saxophone medium. As indicated by its title, *Concertino da Camera* was written as a saxophone solo with the accompaniment of a small (eleven instrument) orchestra. It is usually performed with piano accompaniment, however, and the piano reduction is quite difficult.

Kinyon (arranged), *Breeze-Easy Recital Pieces* (Witmark). This is a collection of well-arranged and appealing solos for the young saxophonist. Both piano and saxophone parts are not difficult. These pieces should afford the student much opportunity for the development of such aspects of musical performance as tone quality, phrasing, and interpretation.

Pierre-Dubois, *Divertissement* (Leduc). This advanced solo is comprised of three movements. The first and third (*allegro vivo* and *scherzando*) stress rapid, precise technique and coordination between tongue and fingers. The middle movement (*lent et doux*) is appropriate for the development of breath support and control, tone quality, and phrasing. An advanced pianist is required for the study and performance of this work.

Rascher (arranged), *The Blue Tail Fly* (Belwin). This is an effective arrangement by one of the leading exponents of saxophone performance and pedagogy. It could well serve as a "first solo" after the student has achieved a fundamental background on the instrument. Both solo and accompaniment are on the easy level.

Teal (arranged), *Solos for the Alto Saxophone Player* (G. Schirmer). This collection includes arrangements of works by Mussorgsky, Schumann, Bach, Dvorak, Mozart and others. The arrangements are both interesting and quite effective for the development of most facets of saxophone performance, including phrasing, breath control, interpretation, articulation, and tone quality. The solos range from the moderately easy to the moderately difficult levels. Their accompaniments are generally not difficult.

Voxman (edited), *Concert and Contest Collection for Eb Alto Saxophone* (Rubank). This well-known and much used collection presents excellent material for the development of the saxophone student. The 14 solos range from easy to moderately difficult, as do their accompaniments. This is a good collection for the development of most aspects of saxophone performance, including phrasing, legato and staccato tonguing, rhythm, rubato playing, and tone quality.

Selected bibliography

Anderson, D. E., "The Controversial Saxophone," *Music Journal*, vol. 17, October, 1959, p. 28.

Cimbalo, L. L., "The Saxophone, Its Development and Use in the School Instrumental Music Program," *Music Educators Journal*, vol. 46, April-May, 1952, p. 38.

Douse, Kenneth, "The Saxophone," *The Instrumentalist*, vol. 2, November, 1947, p. 14.

Gallordoro, Alfred, "Singing on a Sax," *Woodwind World*, vol. 3, January-February, 1959, p. 7.

Holloway, J. H., "He Invented the Saxophone," *Musical Journal*, vol. 18, January, 1960, p. 30.

Mule, Marcel, "The Saxophone," *The Instrumentalist*, vol. 12, April, 1958, p. 30.

Mule, Marcel, "The Saxophone," *Woodwind World*, vol. 1, January, 1958, p. 6.

Opperman, Kalman, *Handbook for Making and Adjusting Single Reeds*. New York, New York: Chappell and Co., 1956.

Pace, Kenneth, "Playing the Saxophone," *The Instrumentalist*, vol. 21, March, 1967, p. 73.

Panhorst, Donald L., "The Saxophone—An Orchestral Instrument," *The Instrumentalist*, vol. 19, November, 1964, p. 43.

Rascher, Sigurd, "The Saxophone Goes to College," *The Instrumentalist*, vol. 19, April, 1965, p. 78.

Rascher, Sigurd, "Thoughts About the Saxophone Mouthpiece," *The Instrumentalist*, vol. 9, October, 1954, p. 18.

Rezits, Joseph, "The Saxophone—A Pianist's Perspective," *Music Journal*, vol. 25, April, 1967, p. 27.

Rousseau, Eugene, "The Interpretation of Jacques Ibert's *Concertion da Camera* for Saxophone," *Woodwind World*, vol. 7, November-December, 1966, p. 5.

Teal, Larry, *The Art of Saxophone Playing*. Evanston, Illinois: Summy-Birchard Company, 1963.

Waln, George, "Saxophone Playing," *The Instrumentalist*, vol. 19, March, 1965, p. 76.

III

TEACHING THE
BRASSES FOR
INDIVIDUAL SKILLS

CHAPTER 11

The Trumpet

The genealogy of the trumpet can be traced to ancient times. Indeed, the first trumpets were probably made from the horns of animals. The slide trumpet appeared during the 17th century, and both the keyed trumpet and the rotary valve instruments were developed in the early 19th century. The piston valve trumpet was invented shortly later, in 1839.

Both the cornet and trumpet contain cylindrical as well as conical tubing. The trumpet, however, has a greater proportion of cylindrical tubing than the cornet. On the other hand, the cornet's bore is not entirely conical because of the cylindrical tubing required for its tuning slides. The tone quality of the trumpet tends to have a certain brilliance about it, while the cornet sound is more mellow. Many directors feel there is little distinction between the two instruments if large-bore trumpets are used. The mouthpiece is also an important factor in enabling the trumpet to produce a mellow sound.

Selecting instructional materials

There is a great deal of instructional literature written for the trumpet in terms of developing the instrumentalist for the high

125

school band. The following is by no means a complete bibliography of trumpet instructional materials. Rather, it is a representative listing which might serve as a guide to the instrumental teacher.

Beginning Methods and Supplementary Studies

Breeze-Easy Method for Trumpet (Kinyon) .... Witmark
(Volumes I and II)

Play Away! (Beeler) .... G. Schirmer

Celebre Method (Arban) .... Leduc
(Volume I)

Graded Lip Trainers (Shuebruk) .... Carl Fischer
(Volume I)

Graded Tongue Trainers (Shuebruk) .... Carl Fischer
(Volume I)

Trumpet Course (Hering) .... Carl Fischer
(Volume I)

Intermediate Methods and Supplementary Studies

Celebre Method (Arban) .... Leduc
(Volume II)

Trumpet Course (Hering) .... Carl Fischer
(Volumes II and III)

Technical Studies (Clarke) .... Carl Fischer

Daily Drills (Schlossberg) .... Baron

Selected Studies for Cornet or Trumpet (Voxman) .... Rubank

Lip Flexibility on the Cornet or Trumpet (Smith) .... Carl Fischer

Graded Lip Trainers (Shuebruk) .... Carl Fischer
(Volumes II and III)

Method for Trumpet (Williams) .... Charles Colin
(Volume I)

Graded Tongue Trainers (Schuebruk) .... Carl Fischer
(Volumes II and III).

Advanced Methods and Supplementary Studies

Celebre Method (Arban) .... Leduc
(Volume III)

Trumpet Course (Hering) .... Carl Fischer
(Volume IV)

Choosing a trumpet, student adaptability, trumpet recordings, and care of the trumpet

Clearly, the aspiring high school trumpeter should have the best instrument available. Of primary consideration should be the tone quality and intonation of the instrument. First-line trumpets are normally tuned to A-440. It should be noted that many of the less expensive instruments have a tendency to be tuned to a higher pitch level. There is also a considerable difference in the tone qualities of first-line instruments as compared to the less expensive models. The first-line trumpet is generally a superior instrument that will perform better over a longer period of time and require less repair work if given proper care. Specifically, the valve action must be smooth and rapid and the slides should move with ease. The instrument should have a quick and easy response in blowing and its tone quality should be both mellow and resonant. If possible a professional trumpet player or brass specialist should check the instrument before it is purchased.

The Mouthpiece. The mouthpiece included with a first-line instrument is usually adequate. Most professionals tend to prefer a good-sized mouthpiece; that is, one with a large cup diameter. This type of mouthpiece allows more air to enter the instrument and should aid in producing a bigger sound. The large cup mouthpiece also permits more of the lip to vibrate. Shallow cup or double cup mouthpieces should normally be avoided. There are numerous trumpet mouthpieces on the market. The student should be encouraged to find a suitable mouthpiece and then remain with it. Constantly changing mouthpieces in the hope of finding the "ideal" is a waste of time, effort, and money. Perhaps of even greater importance, this procedure puts an unusual strain on the player's embouchure. There is no "perfect" mouthpiece and every mouthpiece will involve some adjustment of the embouchure.

In terms of adaptability for the instrument, the student should have a good general intelligence, a strong desire to play the trumpet, and the ability to work diligently at developing his competence. An excessive overbite tends to be somewhat of a handicap in trumpet playing. Relatively thin lips with even upper and lower teeth are desirable physical attributes.

The following recordings are suggested for use in teaching the trumpet:

> "Music for Trumpet and Orchestra," Roger Voisin, Trumpet, KAPP Records #KS 3383 and KS 3384.
>
> "Bram Smith and His Trumpet," Golden Crest record CR 4012.
>
> "The Instruments of the Orchestra" (with narrator and performed by first desk men of the Vienna State Opera Orchestra), Vanguard, records #VRS-1017 and VRS-1018.
>
> "Spotlight on Brass" (Voisin, Meek, and Orosz) VOX, DL300.
>
> "A Trumpet Voluntary in D Major" by Purcell. Samuel Krauss, Trumpet. Columbia #ML 4629.
>
> "Sonata for Trumpet and Piano" by Hindemith. Alex Wilson, Trumpet. EMS 4.
>
> "John Haynie Plays Music for Contest," Austin Custom Record #6502.
>
> "Trumpet Solos," Jack Hyatt, Trumpet. Coronet Program LP #1246.

Cleaning the Trumpet. The trumpet, like any other musical instrument, must receive proper care if it is expected to function at maximum efficiency. It should be cleaned once a week by running warm water through the instrument from the bell end. This should be occasionally supplemented by using soapy water followed by a thorough rinsing with clear water. The valves should be cleaned daily with warm water and then dried with cheesecloth. They should then be lubricated with valve oil manufactured especially for this purpose. The oil should be applied sparingly. The slides should be kept well lubricated with either vaseline or cold cream, and the mouthpiece can be kept clean by using either a mouthpiece brush or a pipe cleaner. Cheesecloth can be used to clean and shine the exterior of the instrument if it is lacquered. Special lacquer cleaners and preservatives are available if desired. Other polishes, such as a high grade silver polish, should be used for cleaning and polishing unlacquered instruments. The student should be thoroughly familiar with the detailed instructions regarding the care of his instrument, which are available from any trumpet manufacturer.

Teaching trumpet playing

The student should sit or stand erect (but relaxed) in order to facilitate good breathing habits as well as a good posture and appearance. The instrument should be held in a horizontal position with the bell pointing forward. The *tips* of the fingers should be used to depress the valves. (See Figure 11-A.) Generally, one-half of the mouthpiece should be placed on the upper lip and the other half on the lower lip. This, however, tends to vary and is largely dependent on the beliefs of the instructor and the physical make-up of the student's teeth and lips. For example, some teach-

Figure 11–A   Trumpet in Playing Position

ers recommend placing one-third of the mouthpiece on the upper lip and two-thirds on the lower lip while others suggest one-third on the lower lip and two-thirds on the upper lip. Excessive pressure of the lips against the mouthpiece should be avoided. This, of course, is not always possible, as in the case of performing music which requires a great deal of volume. (See Figure 11-B.)

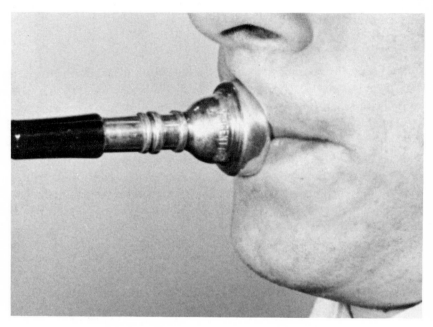

Figure 11–B   Trumpet Embouchure

Trumpet Tone. The concept of tone quality on the trumpet ranges from the heavy, dark German tone to the comparatively thin but brilliant French sound. The majority of American symphonic trumpeters seem to combine the most desirable traits of these two schools. Excellent live performers or fine recordings can be a great aid in helping the student to develop a good "tonal concept" and provide him with a goal for which to strive. In general terms he should seek to produce a solid, compact, but resonant sound that projects well and is euphonic to the ear.

Using Vibrato Correctly. The use of vibrato to embellish the tone should only be developed *after* a fine basic tone quality has been achieved. The vibrato should never be obtrusive or call the listener's attention to it rather than to the basic tone of the instrument. The type of vibrato most commonly employed by trumpet players is the *hand vibrato*. Essentially, this is achieved by a *very slight* back and forth movement of the right hand which causes alternately slight increases and decreases in the amount of lip pressure on the mouthpiece of the instrument. Vibrato is appropriate in lyrical passages. It should, at all times, be used with good taste and discretion and never in an attempt to cover up faulty intonation or a basically poor tone quality.

Teaching Correct Multiple Tonguing. The multiple tonguings (double and triple) are used frequently on the trumpet. (See Figures 11-C and 11-D.)

Figure 11–C

Figure 11–D

They are not difficult to develop and are obviously of great value to the trumpet player. Many brass players have a tendency to exploit these tonguings, however, by using them in passages where they are not really required. The single tongue should be used unless the nature of the music clearly indicates the use of double or triple tonguing techniques. Trumpet players who make a practice of avoiding the use of the single tongue are not, in many cases, able to employ this basic tonguing device very effectively. This is usually due to the deterioration of the single-tongue technique through disuse. This is a regrettable situation since trumpet players usually employ the single tongue to a great extent. It should be kept in mind that the tongue action when pronouncing the syllable "ta" is best for playing in the low range, "tu" for the middle range, and "te" for the high range. Byron Autry points out that, "instead of thinking of the placement of the tip of the tongue it is better to listen carefully to the quality of the 'attack' being produced."[1]

The tongue stroke should always be light and it should also be uniform. Thus, the stroke should be no stronger for unaccented notes than for those that are accented, for *fortissimo* than for *pianissimo,* or for C above the staff than for middle C. The variable element should be the breath velocity and not the tongue stroke.

Intonation problems on the trumpet can result from such factors as low quality instrument, improper breath support and posture, and an undeveloped, weak embouchure. The use of the various valve combinations also tends to affect intonation. For example, all three valves used together produce a *noticeably sharp* pitch. Valves 1 and 3 used together also tend to produce a *noticeably sharp* pitch, whereas valves 1 and 2 tend to produce a *slightly sharp* pitch. Valves 2 and 3 used together usually produce a *slightly flat* pitch. The third valve slide is particularly useful in adjusting the 1–3 and 1–2–3 valve combinations, such as found in C# and D.   Alternate fingerings which can

prove useful and beneficial are:

1. Using the second valve for high C#.
2. Using the 2–3 valve combination if the fourth space Eb is flat. (This will sometimes also require adjusting with the third valve slide.)
3. Using the third valve to eliminate possible sharpness frequently found on first line E.

4. Using the third valve for the high A   in the event that the usual 1–2 combination is sharp.

[1]Byron Autry, "Cornet" in *Building Better Bands* (Rockville Centre, L.I., New York: Belwin, Inc., 1957), p. 20.

A large bore mouthpiece with a deep cup has a tendency to make the player sound flat, whereas a shallow cup mouthpiece with a small bore in the mouthpiece will tend to cause the player to sound sharp.[2] As a prime prerequisite for improving intonation on the trumpet, the student must possess good pitch sensitivity. Good posture with deep diaphragmatic breathing, resulting both in good breath support and breath control, are also factors related to the improvement of intonation. A *first-line* instrument tuned to A-440 and well in tune within itself is a great asset in achieving good intonation on the trumpet. The instrument should have a trigger mechanism attached to the first valve slide and a ring attached to the third valve slide for tuning purposes. Alternate fingerings are also used to improve intonation and, to some extent, pitches can be altered by means of adjusting the embouchure. A well-developed, strong embouchure would also seem to be closely related to the ability to play the trumpet in tune.

Trumpet Lip Slurs. The playing of lip slurs should be part and parcel of every trumpet player's daily practice routine. The so-called lip slur consists, for the most part, of the flow of breath into the instrument and the fluctuation of this flow of breath by employment of the back portion of the player's tongue. The player should take note of the tongue's position when he whistles various intervals such as thirds, fourths, sixths, and the like. Two syllables suggested for altering the position of the back area of the tongue are "e" for the upper tones and "ah" for the lower tones. For example, when slurring from second space A to fourth space E the movement of the tongue should be "ta-e." When slurring back down the tongue movement should be "te-ah."[3]

Finally, a word needs to be said about the physical conditioning of the brass player. Perhaps one reason this is seldom discussed is that it is usually taken for granted. Actually, many musicians appear to get very little physical exercise. Yet it seems reasonable to assume that a certain amount of physical conditioning is quite essential for the effective execution of any profession. Maurice Faulkner points out that: "My research over the past decade or more has indicated that brass instrumentalists need to

---

[2]Daryl J. Gibson, *A Textbook for Trumpet* (Minneapolis: T. S. Denison and Company, Inc., 1962), p. 11.
[3]Autry, p. 20.

be concerned with keeping in top physical condition."[4] There are now available several books dealing with physical fitness. One of the best is *Physical Fitness and Dynamic Health* by Dr. Thomas K. Cureton, Jr. (Dial Press, New York City). In an age when so many people find themselves engaged in sedentary occupations there seems to be an increasing interest in the area of physical conditioning.

A selected and annotated list of trumpet solo literature for the development of specific individual skills

Anderson, *A Trumpeter's Lullaby* (Mills). This is but one of Leroy Anderson's fine solos for the less experienced trumpet player. (Others include *Bugler's Holiday, Blue Tango,* and *The Music of Leroy Anderson* [collection] all published by Mills.) These solos are especially appealing to the young player and are generally on the moderately easy level as are their accompaniments. Most aspects of trumpet pedagogy and performance can be developed within the framework of these solos.

Arban, *The Carnival of Venice* (Cundy-Bettoney). *The Carnival of Venice* is a work with which nearly all trumpet players are familiar. It is essentially a display piece for this instrument and requires an advanced performer with an unusually good technical command of his instrument. This work requires much in the areas of tonguing, control, technique, breath support, and performing in the high range of the trumpet. The accompaniment is not greatly demanding.

Contemporary French Recital Pieces (International). Included in this collection are works by Semenoff, Jolivet, Lesur, Pascal and others. They are generally of short duration, cleverly written, and make good recital material. Their levels of difficulty suggest advanced students on both the trumpet and the piano.

Correli-Fitzgerald, *Sonata No. VIII* (Leeds). This is an effective transcription of a well-known Correli sonata. It could serve to acquaint the moderately advanced trumpet student with the baroque period of musical literature. The "Prelude" and "Sarabande" emphasize smooth legato playing, breath control, and phrasing. The "Sarabande"

---

[4]Maurice Faulkner, "Physical Fitness for Brass Players," *The Instrumentalist,* September, 1967, p. 46.

requires accuracy in tone placement during rather wide skips in the notation as well as a good command of some of the higher notes on the trumpet. The "Gigue" stresses precise, accurate technique as well as fluency in the higher range. The accompaniment is also on the moderately advanced level.

Haydn, *Concerto for Trumpet* (G. Schirmer). Nearly every advanced trumpet student studies this well-known work. It is one of the few trumpet compositions from the classical period of musical literature. As a prerequisite for the study of the Haydn *Concerto* the student should have achieved a rather high level of musical maturity in addition to adequate technical facility on his instrument. The piano reduction, while not exceedingly difficult, requires a sensitive and advanced performer.

Hindemith, *Sonata for Trumpet and Piano* (Associated). Completed in 1939, this is one of Hindemith's better and more ambitious instrumental sonatas. A technically advanced and musically mature high school student should be able to profit from the study and performance of this work. As is the case with most contemporary sonatas, the piano part is vitally important to the understanding of the sonata as a whole, and an advanced performer is also required on this instrument.

Hovhaness, *Prayer of St. Gregory* (Southern). This solo is in the contemporary English idiom and is on the moderately easy level. It is a slow, lyrical work and would seem to be especially appropriate for the development of phrasing, tone quality, extension of range, and breath support. The piano accompaniment is not difficult.

Kinyon (arr.), *Breeze-Easy Recital Pieces* (Witmark). This is a good collection for the trumpet player about to embark on the study of solo literature. Most of the pieces in this collection are well known and both trumpet and piano parts are on the easy level. These solos should aid in the development of tone production, breath support, intonation, phrasing, and interpretation.

Laube (arr.), *Contest Album for Cornet and Piano* (Cundy-Bettoney). This is a collection of solos selected by the National Contest Committee, some of which were originally written for the Paris Conservatory. Included are works by Gaubert, Alary, Mouquet, Busser, and others. The solos and their accompaniments are on the moderately advanced to advanced levels.

Lawton (arr.), *The Young Trumpet Player* (Oxford). This collection is available in three volumes. Volume I is comprised largely of hymns and folksongs, most of which are on the easy level. These are particularly appropriate for the inexperienced trumpet student to study and develop his tone quality and breath support. Volumes II and III contain effective transcriptions of works by such composers as Purcell, Handel, and Clark. The levels of difficulty found in volumes II and III range from moderately easy to moderately difficult. They can be used to advantage in the development of most aspects of musicianship on the trumpet, including the extension of range, rhythm, tone production, phrasing, staccato and legato playing, and technical facility. The accompaniments are generally not prohibitive.

Levy-Buchtel, *Grand Russian Fantasia* (Kjos). *Grand Russian Fantasia* is an impressive solo on the moderately advanced level. It would seem to be especially appropriate for the development of a technical command of the instrument as well as for the development of multiple-tonguing technique. The accompaniment is not as difficult as the solo part.

Mager (arr.), *Nine Grands Solos de Concert for Trumpet and Piano* (Southern). This collection is comprised of contemporary French solos revised by the former solo trumpet player of the Boston Symphony Orchestra. Included are works by Hüe, Thomè, Balay, Savard and others. This is a valuable group of solos for the development of the moderately advanced to advanced trumpet student. The accompaniments are also on these levels of difficulty.

Ropartz-Mager, *Andante et Allegro* (Southern). This is another effective solo that should require a moderately advanced student for performance. The slow opening section stresses phrasing, breath control, and a smooth, legato-style playing. The allegro sections involve a considerable amount of tonguing as well as accuracy of pitch placement, breath support, and performance in the upper register of the instrument. The accompaniment is also on the moderately advanced level.

Voxman (edited), *Concert and Contest Collection for Trumpet* (Rubank). Included in this collection are works by Barat, Ostransky, Clerisse, Maniet and others. The technical and musical difficulty of these solos places them on the moderately easy to moderately difficult levels. This is a good collection for the high school trumpet student. The solos found in this book can be used to advantage in the development of most aspects of musicianship on the trumpet including the extension of range, tone production, rhythm, technical facility, tonguing, and interpretation. The accompaniments also range from moderately easy to moderately difficult.

Selected bibliography

Autry, Byron, "Cornet" in *Building Better Bands*. Rockville Centre, L.I., New York: Belwin, Inc., 1957.

Bach, Vincent, "The Art of Trumpet Playing," *Selmer Bandwagon*, vol. 15, April, 1967, p. 16.

Bach, Vincent, "How to Choose the Best Mouthpiece Cup," *Selmer Bandwagon*, vol. 14, May, 1966, p. 16.

Bach, Vincent, "Know Your Brasses," *Selmer Bandwagon*, vol. 15, April, 1967, p. 4.

Bach, Vincent, "Notes on Instrument Design," *Selmer Bandwagon*, vol. 15, April, 1967, p. 10.

Bate, Philip, *The Trumpet and Trombone*. New York, New York: W. W. Norton & Company, Inc., 1966.

Bush, Irving R., *Artistic Trumpet Technique and Study*. Hollywood, California: Highland Music Company, 1962.

Colin, Charles, *Vital Brass Notes*. Kenosha,Wisconsin: G. Leblanc Corporation, 1955.

Dale, Delbert A., *Trumpet Technique*. New York, New York: Oxford University Press, 1965.

Ehmann, Wilhelm, "New Brass Instruments Based on Old Models," *Brass Quarterly*, vol. 1, June, 1958, p. 214.

Farkas, Philip, *The Art of Brass Playing*. Bloomington, Indiana: Brass Publications, 1962.

Faulkner, Maurice, "Physical Fitness for Brass Players," *The Instrumentalist*, vol. 22, September, 1967, p. 46.

Getchell, Robert, *Teacher's Guide to the Brass Instruments*, Elkhart, Indiana: H. & A. Selmer Inc., 1959.

Gibson, Daryl J., *A Textbook for Trumpet*. Minneapolis, Minnesota: T. S. Denison & Company, Inc., 1962.

Hanson, Fay, *Brass Playing, the Mechanism and the Technic*, New York, New York: Carl Fischer, Inc., 1968.

Haynie, John J., "A Graded List of Trumpet Solos," *The Instrumentalist*, vol. 18, August, 1963, p. 47.

Hoover, Cynthia Adams, "The Slide Trumpet of the Nineteenth Century," *Brass Quarterly*, vol. 6, Summer, 1963, p. 159.

Neilson, James, *Warm-Up Procedures for the Brass Player*. Kenosha, Wisconsin: G. Leblanc Corporation, 1962.

Noble, Clyde E., *The Psychology of Cornet and Trumpet Playing*. Missoula, Montana: Montana State University Press, 1964.

Rasmussen, Mary, *A Teacher's Guide to the Literature of Brass Instruments*. Durham, New Hampshire: *Brass Quarterly*, 1964.

Severinsen, Carl, "Why Warm Up?" *The School Musician*, vol. 39, August-September, 1967, p. 68.

Stanley, Donald A., "Style in Brass Playing," *National Association of College Wind and Percussion Instructors Bulletin*, vol. 15, Fall, 1966, p. 10.

Stauffer, Donald W., *Intonation Deficiencies of Wind Instruments in Ensemble*. Washington, D.C.: The Catholic University of America Press, 1954.

Sweeney, Leslie, *Teaching Techniques for the Brasses*. Rockville Center, Long Island, New York: Belwin, Inc., 1953.

Turrentine, Edgar M., "The Trumpet's Day," *The Instrumentalist*, vol. 19, March, 1965, p. 72.

Weast, Robert D., *Brass Performance*. New York, New York: McGinnis & Marx, 1962.

Winslow, Robert W. and John E. Green, *Playing and Teaching Brass Instruments*. Englewood Cliffs, New Jersey: Prentice-Hall, Inc., 1961.

Winter, James H., *The Brass Instruments*. Boston, Massachusetts: Allyn and Bacon, Inc., 1964.

Whitaker, Donald, "Trumpet and Cornet Recordings," *National Association of College Wind and Percussion Instructors Bulletin*, vol. 12, June, 1964, p. 23.

Whitaker, Donald, "Brass Recordings," *The Instrumentalist*, vol. 20, June, 1966, p. 73.

CHAPTER 12

The French Horn

When considered as a musical instrument the horn has a relatively short history. It was probably first used in an orchestral setting during the early 1700's. The horn with crooks appeared shortly thereafter, and the keyed horn was first used about 1760. The valved horns were developed in the early 1800's and the Kruspe Company produced the first double horn in the late nineteenth century.

The horn is both one of the most difficult and one of the most versatile brass instruments. Composers have used its euphonic sound to blend with various woodwind, brass, and vocal combinations. From the student's point of view, the horn is both challenging and rewarding. From the band director's viewpoint a fine horn section is a most valuable asset to his organization.

Selecting instructional materials

There is a great abundance of excellent instructional literature written for the development of the French horn player, and much of this material has been written by seasoned performers on the instrument. The following representative listing is intended to serve as a guide for the instrumental teacher.

Beginning Methods and Supplementary Studies

Breeze-Easy Method for the French Horn (Kinyon) ..... Witmark
First Book of Practical Studies for the French Horn
(Getchell) .... Belwin
Method for French Horn (Howe) .... Remick
Elementary Method for French Horn (Skornicka) .... Rubank
Supplementary Studies for French Horn (Endresen) .... Rubank
Pares Scales for French Horn .... Rubank
Primary Studies for the French Horn (Horner) .... Elkan-Vogel
200 Modern French Horn Etudes, Books 1 and 2
(Maxime-Alphonse) .... Leduc
Fundamental Method for French Horn .... Universal

Intermediate Methods and Supplementary Studies

Intermediate Method (Skornicka-Erdman) .... Rubank
Advanced Method, Volumes I and II (Voxman-Gower) .... Rubank
Second Book of Practical Studies for French Horn
(Getchell) .... Belwin
Preparatory Melodies to Solo Work for French Horn
(ed. Pottag) .... Belwin
Complete Method for the French Horn (Thévet),
Volumes I and II .... Leduc
200 Modern French Horn Etudes, Book 3
(Maxime-Alphonse) .... Leduc
Thirteen Etudes for French Horn (Weber) .... Leduc

Advanced Methods and Supplementary Studies

Forty-Eight Etudes for French Horn (Reynolds) .... G. Schirmer
Twelve Etudes for French Horn (Bitsch) .... Leduc
Fifteen Etudes for French Horn (Chaynes) .... Leduc
200 Modern French Horn Etudes, Books 4, 5, and 6
(Maxime-Alphonse) .... Leduc
Sixty Studies (Kopprasch) .... Cundy-Bettoney
Twelve Etudes for French Horn (Muller) .... Sansone

Choosing a French horn, student adaptability, French horn recordings, and care of the French horn

The French horn is one of the instruments frequently owned by the school system. It is decidedly to the best interest of the school system, as well as the band director, to purchase first-line instruments. From a strictly business point of view, first-line instruments are usually a much better buy than the less expensive models. It is also wise to purchase double horns (in F and B♭) rather than single horns in these keys. The double horn combines all of the advantages of the two single horns and is by far the most popular instrument among French horn players. The double horn is a more expensive instrument but is of more value to both the student and the school instrumental organizations. In addition to its three usual valves, this instrument also has a fourth valve which is operated by the thumb. This valve, when depressed, eliminates the necessary amount of tubing to put the horn into the key of B♭, a perfect fourth higher than the F horn. Although horn players do not always change from the F horn to the B♭ horn on the same note, the change will usually occur be-

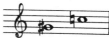

tween G# and C in the treble clef.   The five half-tones found within this interval are fingered in an identical manner on both the F and B♭ horns. As a rule notes *below* the G# are played on the F side of the instrument and notes *above* the C are played on the B♭ side. As the student becomes more advanced, he should learn both the F and B♭ fingerings for the entire range of the horn.[1]

The valve action should be smooth and rapid and the horn should have an easy response in blowing. Its tone should be idiomatic and pleasing to the ear. If possible, a professional horn player or brass specialist should check the instruments before they are purchased.

Selecting the Mouthpiece. There are numerous kinds of horn mouthpieces on the market and the student can waste a great deal of time, money, and effort looking for the "ideal" mouthpiece. Farkas offers the following advice regarding French horn mouthpieces:

> The best advice about mouthpieces, stated in capsule form, would be this: get a mouthpiece which is generally accepted as "normal." (Conn Number 2, Bach Number 7, Reynolds 6D, King H-2, Farkas-Model, are all good examples.) It

[1]Robert Getchell, *Teacher's Guide to the Brass Instruments* (Elkhart, Indiana: H. & A. Selmer, Inc., 1959), p. 18–19.

takes experience to know what "normal" is, but study two dozen different models and you will soon recognize moderation. Be sure the one you choose has no obviously bad qualities; make certain it is comfortable on the lips; then stick with it until it is mastered.[2]

The selection of the French horn student is of considerable importance since this instrument is generally regarded to be one of the most difficult musical instruments. It is undoubtedly advantageous for the prospective horn student to have had some musical training prior to studying the horn. He should have average intelligence and better-than-average musical talent and perseverance to do well on this instrument. It is obviously mandatory that he be able to hear intervals and intervalic interrelationships with precision and accuracy. Physically, average size lips and straight teeth are helpful. Exceedingly small, thin lips or lips that are large and flabby tend to militate against achieving success on the French horn.

The following recordings are suggested for use in teaching the French horn:

> *Concertos No. 1, 2, 3,* and *4* by Mozart. Dennis Brain, French Horn. Angel Record #35092.
>
> "French Horn Solos," Philip Farkas, French Horn. Coronet Program LP #1293.
>
> John Barrows, French Horn. (French Horn Sonatas) Golden Crest Record #7002.
>
> Joseph Eger, French Horn. (Solo and Ensemble Literature) RCA Record #2146.
>
> William Chambers, French Horn. (Solo Literature) Award Record #704.
>
> Joseph Stagliano, French Horn. (The Four Mozart *Concertos*) Boston Record #401.
>
> "Spotlight on Brass," (Voisin, Meek, and Orosz) VOX, DL 300.
>
> "The Art of Dennis Brain." Seraphim Record #60040.
>
> "Larghetto for Horn and Orchestra," by Chabrier. Mason Jones, French Horn. Columbia #ML 4629.

---

[2]Philip Farkas, *The Art of French Horn Playing* (Evanston, Illinois: Summy-Birchard Publishing Company, 1956), p. 5.

Proper Care of the French Horn. If given adequate care, the French horn can function well for long periods of time with only minor repairs. The slides should be kept well lubricated with either vaseline or cold cream. The rotary valves are of major importance when considering the care of the French horn. These valves should be oiled frequently from both the top and bottom. The rotary valves should normally be taken apart and cleaned only by a professional repairman. Replacing the valve strings is not a complicated procedure and several of these strings (already tied) should be kept in readiness. Since the French horn has no water key, water should frequently be drained from the slides and other tubing. The bell area of most horns is made of thin, soft metal and special care should be taken to avoid damaging this part of the instrument. The mouthpiece should be carried in a pouch or case in order to avoid damage. When putting the horn in its case care should be taken to make certain that it is securely blocked and strapped. Books, music, and other items should not be carried in the case. Complete instructions regarding the care and maintenance of the French horn are available from any manufacturer of this instrument. A very good general booklet is the Conn publication, *How to Care for Your Instrument.*

Teaching French horn playing

A good embouchure is particularly important in French horn performance due to the accuracy problem inherent in this instrument. While there should be a *slight smile* there should also be an obvious contraction of the muscles toward the center of the lips. Some students have a tendency to let their cheeks puff out as they play. It is, of course, possible to correct this imperfection *up to a point.* If this fundamentally bad habit is allowed to develop it will almost surely result in loss of accuracy and control on the instrument. The mouthpiece should be horizontally centered on the lips with about two-thirds on the upper lip and one-third on the lower lip. Clearly, there will have to be adjustments made during register shifts, but these should be kept to a minimum. If there is any adjustment of embouchure to facilitate wide range, it should involve only the upper lip. The mouthpiece should remain stationary on the lower lip. Excessive pressure on the mouthpiece should be avoided. (See Figures 12-A and 12-B.)

Figure 12–A   French Horn in Playing Position

Figure 12–B   French Horn Embouchure

Flexibility of attack is probably best for the French horn players. When the part (or conductor) demands precision and crispness "tah" is best. When the part is more lyrical "da" is usually best.

Hand-in-Bell Techniques. The tone quality of this instrument can be considerably altered by both the embouchure and the hand in the bell. For example, an excessively "smiling" type embouchure tends to produce a rather brilliant, "brassy" tone. On the other hand, the more the hand is cupped and the bell closed the darker the tone quality becomes. The reverse produces a bright sound. Every advanced horn player undoubtedly has his own distinctive tone quality. Listening to fine professional performers on this instrument, either live or on record, is very helpful in the development of a tonal concept. Vibrato is rarely used on the French horn and is not recommended.

As the prime prerequisite to achieving good intonation on the French horn the student must have a fine sense of pitch. Assuming this, probably the greatest single intonation aid to horn players is the hand in the bell. Obviously, the further the hand is put into the bell, the flatter the pitch becomes. Conversely, the more open the bell, the sharper the pitch. Some pitch adjustment is possible with the embouchure and alternate fingerings. In some cases alternating between the F and B*b* horns will improve the intonation of certain tones.

Single horns are manufactured with one principal tuning slide, while the double horn has two. The horn, single or double, should first be tuned with the principal slide or slides and with the right hand in its usual playing position in the instrument's bell. After the principal tuning slide (or slides) has been used to tune the open horn the individual valve slides should be tuned. Usually the horns are built a bit on the sharp side when the valves are entirely in. They should, therefore, be pulled out in direct relation to their length. This would mean that the third valve would have to be pulled the most, the second the least, and the first a bit more than the second. Many horn players mark both the tuning slides and valve slides for easy and rapid replacement following the emptying of condensation. A minor adjustment in the principal tuning slide should not require an adjustment of the valve slides.[3]

---

[3]Norman J. Hunt, *Guide to Teaching Brass* (Dubuque, Iowa: Wm. C. Brown Company Publishers, 1968), p. 44.

Various composers have indicated the use of "stopped horn." Essentially, this involves putting the right hand into the bell in an effort to cut off *all* air. This, of course, is not entirely possible, but when it is properly executed the pitch of the instrument is *raised a half step* thus requiring the player to transpose *down a half step*. (See Figures 12-C and 12-D.) When *muting* is indicated, a non-transposing type mute is used, such as the kind made from metal, wood, or cardboard. A "transposing mute" is available for those players who have considerable difficulty in hand-stopping the horn.

Principles of Transposition. Numerous horn parts are scored for instruments pitched in keys either lower or higher than the two horns which comprise the double horn. These would include horns in A, G, E, E*b*, D, and C. Every fairly advanced horn student should be aware of the principles involved in transposition since it is used so extensively on the horn. Two of the most common transpositions are to horns in E and E*b*. In the former the student thinks in terms of playing all notation *down one-half step*. In the latter case all notation is played *down one full step*. This is accomplished by *interval transposition* since the intervals involved are essentially small.

In the case of the larger intervals, *clef transposition* is usually employed. For example, to transpose to horn in C the *baritone*

clef   is used; that is, this clef is substituted for the written treble clef. Developing fluency in transposition requires considerable skill and practice. It is, however, important in advanced French horn playing.

A selected and annotated list of French horn solo literature for the development of specific individual skills

Bach-Vuillermoz, *Aria* (Leduc). This is a very effective arrangement of a much-performed Bach work. It is especially effective for the development of breath support, phrasing, tone production, and control. Technically, this solo is not difficult and the notation is well within the middle range of the horn. Both horn and piano parts are on the moderately advanced level.

Beethoven, *Sonata for French Horn*, Opus 17 (Carl Fischer). This

Figure 12–C   French Horn Hand in the Bell, Normal Position

Figure 12–D   French Horn Hand in the Bell, Stopped-Horn Position

sonata is comprised of three movements—two rather extensive fast movements separated by a brief slow movement. A wide range of notation is employed with frequent wide skips requiring control and accuracy of pitch placement. Legato, portato, and staccato tonguing are all used in the work. The solo part is on the moderately advanced level, and the piano part is technically more demanding than the horn part.

Händel-Reynolds, *Third Sonata* (Southern). This is an effective although difficult transcription. The first and third movements, "Adagio" and "Largo," are particularly well suited for the development of breath control and phrasing. The "Allegro" second and fourth movements require a considerable amount of technique and control. The horn part is on the advanced level while the piano part requires a moderately advanced performer.

Händel-Vuillermoz, *Largo* (Leduc). The notation of this solo is largely diatonic in nature and its technical demands are modest. Considerable breath support is required, however. It is also an effective solo for the development of phrasing and playing at widely different dynamic levels. Both parts are on the moderately easy level. A harpsichord, if available, should be used in lieu of the piano.

Haydn, *Concertos No. 1* and *2 for French Horn* (Cundy-Bettoney). Every serious horn student should study these works from the classical period of musical literature. Their technical and musical difficulty places them on the advanced level. *Concerto No. 1* requires considerable fluency in the high range of the instrument, while many wide skips in notation are found in the second *Concerto*. These concertos are appropriate for the development of all aspects of musical performance on the French horn. Their piano reductions require advanced performers on this instrument.

Heiden, *Sonata for Horn and Piano* (Associated). Completed in 1939, this work somewhat resembles the general style of Hindemith. It is idiomatically written for the instrument and appropriate for the development of the advanced high school French horn student. As is the case with most contemporary sonatas, the piano part is quite important to the understanding of the sonata as a whole and an advanced performer on this instrument is also required.

Hindemith, *Concerto for French Horn* (Associated). This is one of the best of the contemporary concertos for the French horn. Completed in 1949, the Hindemith *Concerto* requires a technically advanced and musically mature high school student. The piano reduction is also on the difficult level.

Jones (edited), *Solos for the Horn Player* (G. Schirmer). This collection includes adaptations of works by such composers as Haydn, Ropartz, Handel, Mozart, Adam, and others. The arrangements are both interesting and effective for the development of most facets of French horn performance, including breath control, phrasing, interpretation, articulation, intonation, pitch placement, and tone quality. The solos range from the moderately easy to the moderately difficult levels. Their accompaniments are generally not difficult.

Kinyon (arr.), *Breeze-Easy Recital Pieces for Horn in F* (Witmark). This is a good first solo book for the young French horn player. Most of the included solos are well known and the accompaniments are quite easy. Two other books which fall into this same general category are: *82 French Horn Solos* (arr.) published by Belwin and *The Young Artist's First Book of Solos* (Buchtel) published by Cole. The solos found in these books can be used to advantage for the development of most aspects of musicianship on the French horn, including tone production, phrasing, breath support, control of pitch, and interpretation.

Mendelssohn-Vuillermoz, *Romance Sans Paroles* (Leduc). This solo is another example of an effective and musical adaptation to the French horn medium. The notation is scored, for the most part, in the instrument's middle range. A considerable amount of breath support is required. *Romance Sans Paroles* is also appropriate for the development of dynamic control and phrasing. Both horn and piano parts are on the moderately advanced level of difficulty.

Mozart, *Concertos No. 1*, (K. 412) *2*, (K. 417) *3*, (K. 447) and *4* (K. 495). (G. Schirmer). Many professional horn teachers and performers feel that these concertos should be studied on the college level. Actually, a mature high school student can probably profit from these works if he has achieved a considerable amount of technical facility and musical maturity on his instrument. The piano reductions also require a sensitive and advanced performer.

Pergolese-Vuillermoz, *Sicilienne* (Leduc). This is a very musical adaptation which requires only a modest amount of technical facility. It does, however, provide much opportunity for the development of phrasing, tone production, intonation, and dynamic control. Both horn and piano parts are on the intermediate level of difficulty.

Saint-Säens-Voxman, *Romance* (Rubank). *Romance* is a very melodic and euphonic solo on the intermediate level of difficulty. It is well adapted to the French horn medium and the notation lies in the middle range of the instrument. It is a slow, lyrical work which would seem to be especially appropriate for the development of phrasing, accuracy of pitch placement, tone production, and breath support. The piano accompaniment is not difficult.

Scarmolin, *Romanza and Allegro* (Pro Art). Technically, this solo is not greatly demanding. Its pitch range is also not excessive and the intermediate French horn student should be able to concentrate on such aspects of performance as accurate pitch placement, tone quality, breath control, and phrasing. The accompaniment is also on the intermediate level.

Strauss, *Concerto for French Horn*, Opus 11 (Cundy-Bettoney). Every advanced horn student eventually studies this well-known horn concerto. It is a fine Romantic work and displays the potential of the horn quite well. This concerto requires an advanced performer with an unusually good technical command of his instrument. It demands much in the areas of control, breath support, technique, and performing in both the high and low ranges of the French horn. The piano reduction is also on the difficult level.

Strauss-Voxman, *Allerseelen* (Rubank). This is an effective first solo for the neophyte horn student. The notation is largely confined to the low-middle range of the instrument. Its technical demands are modest, thus providing the student opportunity to concentrate on such aspects of performance as accuracy of pitch placement, tone quality, breath support, and phrasing. The accompaniment is also on the easy level.

Wiedemann-Pottag, *Nocturno* (Belwin). This is a well-written solo for the development of the intermediate French horn student. It should aid in the extension of the player's range, although the range per se is not prohibitive. Several ornamentive devices are used as trills, turns, and grace notes. Much of the notation is either diatonic or quasi-diatonic. The accompaniment is also on the intermediate level.

Voxman (edited), *Concert and Contest Collection for French Horn in F* (Rubank). The technical and musical difficulty of these solos places them on the moderately easy to moderately advanced levels. The solos found in this book are appropriate for use in the development of most aspects of musicianship on the French horn including extension of range, rhythm, tone production, technical facility, legato and staccato tonguing, phrasing, and interpretation. The accompaniments also range from moderately easy to moderately difficult.

Selected bibliography

Chambers, James, "Horn Tone and Technique," *Woodwind World*, vol. 4, June, 1962, p. 11.

Crain, Robert C., "For Better Horn Players," *The Instrumentalist*, vol. 21, January, 1967, p. 53.

Farkas, Philip, *The Art of Brass Playing*. Bloomington, Indiana: Brass Publications, 1962.

Farkas, Philip, *The Art of French Horn Playing*. Evanston, Illinois: Summy-Birchard Publishing Company, 1956.

Faulkner, Maurice, "Brass Tone Color," *The Instrumentalist*, vol. 19, January, 1965, p. 51.

Getchell, Robert, *Teacher's Guide to the Brass Instruments*. Elkhart, Indiana: H. & A. Selmer, Inc., 1959.

Gregory, Robin, *The Horn*. London: Faber and Faber, 1961.

Hunt, Norman J., *Guide to Teaching Brass*. Dubuque, Iowa: Wm. C. Brown Company, 1968.

Johnson, Merton B., "Muting the French Horn," *The Instrumentalist*, vol. 19, January, 1965, p. 51.

Leidig, Vernon F., *Contemporary Brass Technique*. Hollywood, California: Highland Music Company, 1960.

Magnell, Elmer, "Horn in F or B-flat?" *The Instrumentalist*, vol. 17, October, 1962, p. 66.

McConathy, Osborne, "Great Horn Virtuosi of the Past," *Woodwind World*, vol. 3, September, 1959, p. 14.

Neilson, James, *Breathing and Breath Control*. Kenosha, Wisconsin: G. Leblanc Corporation, 1962.

Neilson, James, *The Overtone Principle*. Kenosha, Wisconsin: G. Leblanc Corporation, 1962.

Neilson, James, *Warm-Up Procedures for the Brass Player*. Kenosha, Wisconsin: G. Leblanc Corporation, 1962.

Rasmussen, Mary, *A Teacher's Guide to the Literature of Brass Instruments*. Durham, New Hampshire: *Brass Quarterly*, 1964.

Schuller, Gunther, *Horn Technique*. New York, New York: Oxford University Press, 1962.

Silliman, A. Cutler, "The Double Horn," *The Instrumentalist*, vol. 17, March, 1963, p. 81.

Silliman, A. Cutler, "Low Register of the French Horn," *The Instrumentalist*, vol. 17, November, 1962, p. 62.

Silliman, A. Cutler, "Technical Problems on the Double Horn," *The Instrumentalist*, vol. 18, January, 1964, p. 82.

Winslow, Robert W. and John E. Green, *Playing and Teaching Brass Instruments*. Englewood Cliffs, New Jersey: Prentice-Hall, Inc., 1961.

Winter, James H., *The Brass Instruments*. Boston, Mass.: Allyn and Bacon, Inc., 1964.

Winter, James H., "Concerning the "Ring" in Horn Tone," *Woodwind World*, vol. 5, June, 1964, p. 5.

Winter, James H., "The French Horn Mouthpiece," *Woodwind World*, vol. 6, September, 1964, p. 3.

Winter, James H., "Pianissimo Control," *National Association of College Wind and Percussion Instructors Bulletin*, vol. 13, Spring, 1965, p. 5.

Yancich, Milan, "Philip Farkas and the French Horn," *Woodwind World*, vol. 4, February, 1963, p. 10.

CHAPTER 13

The Trombone

Although historical authorities are far from concurrence regarding a specific date of origin, it is probable that a predecessor of the trombone first appeared in Italy during the early 15th century. One of the early uses of the trombone in a musical composition was by Gabrieli in the later part of the 16th century.

This cylindrical-bored instrument functions within a range of approximately three octaves. Although the majority of notation scored for the trombone is in the bass clef, the tenor clef is rather extensively used, particularly in advanced étude material and orchestral work. The alto clef is less frequently employed in the scoring of trombone music.

Selecting instructional materials

The available instructional literature written for the trombone is not as comprehensive and inclusive as that written for some of the other brass instruments. It is, adequate, however, and more is continually becoming available. The following is a selective and representative listing of étude material for the development of the trombone student.

Beginning Methods and Supplementary Studies

Method for the Trombone (Beeler) (Volume I) .... Remick
Elementary Method for Trombone (Long) .... Rubank
Breeze-Easy Method for Trombone (Kinyon) .... Witmark
Play Away! (Beeler) .... G. Schirmer
Pares Scales for Trombone (Pares-Whistler) .... Rubank
Supplementary Studies for Trombone (Endresen) .... Rubank

Intermediate Methods and Supplementary Studies

221 Progressive Studies (Cimera) .... Belwin
Etudes for Trombone (Vandercook-Welke) .... Rubank
Method for the Trombone (Beeler) (Volume II) .... Remick
Intermediate Method for Trombone (Skornicka-Boltz) .... Rubank
Advanced Method for Trombone (Gower-Voxman)
   (Volumes I and II) .... Rubank
Selected Studies for Trombone (Voxman) .... Rubank
Complete Method for Trombone (Lafosse)
   (Volume I) .... Leduc
Clef Studies for Trombone (Blazhevich) .... Leeds
Melodious Etudes for Trombone (Bordogni-Rochut)
   (Volume I) .... Carl Fischer

Advanced Methods and Supplementary Studies

Complete Method for Trombone (Lafosse) .... Leduc
Melodious Etudes for Trombone (Bordogni-Rochut
(Volumes II and III) .... Carl Fischer
36 Studies for Trombone with F Attachment
   (Blume-Fink) .... Carl Fischer
Develop Sight Reading (Dufresne-Voisin) .... Colin
26 Melodic Studies in Varied Rhythms and Keys
   (Blazhevich) .... Carl Fischer
15 Rhythmic Etudes (Bitsch) .... Leduc

Choosing a trombone, student adaptability, trombone recordings, and care of the trombone

The same high standards of workmanship and construction applicable in the selection of other brass instruments also apply to the trombone. The instrument should have an easy response in blowing, good tone quality, and pitch stability. Probably the most important single aspect to consider when selecting a trombone is its slide. Ecker recommends the following method for testing the trombone slide:

To test a trombone slide, open the lock and lower the slide until the bow rests on the floor. Pull the slide upward by plugging one opening with your thumb and sucking on the other like a drinking straw. The slide should hop quickly into closed position. Use only a dry slide in making this test.[1]

Although the standard tenor trombone is still probably the most widely used trombone, many players tend to prefer this instrument with an F attachment. The two chief advantages of the F attachment are the extension of the low register and the added technical facility which this device affords. Actually, there is very little difference between the tenor trombone with F attachment and the present day bass trombone. The bass trombone does, however, have a somewhat larger bore size and many band directors prefer this instrument for the low (third) trombone parts.

A relatively recent innovation has been the introduction of the tenor trombone with G attachment. This attachment does not extend the range of the tenor trombone. Rather, its chief advantage is that it essentially eliminates the necessity of using all positions beyond the fourth, thus making the trombone more readily accessible to younger students and adults with shorter arms. When selecting a trombone, it should again be pointed out that much frustration can be avoided and money saved by purchasing a first-line instrument.

A standard mouthpiece is recommended rather than one which has radical construction of bore, rim cup, or backbore. Winter suggests that, "Standard mouthpieces such as the Vincent Bach 6 and 7 series, or the H.N. White M-21 and M-31 should be used."[2] He further comments: "Unfortunately, there are almost as many freak mouthpieces for the trombone as there are for the trumpet; they are no better for the one than for the other."[3] Since the bass trombone has larger tubing than the tenor trombone a larger mouthpiece should be used for this instrument. "Extension-receivers" are available which adapt the standard trombone mouthpiece to the mouthpipe of the bass trombone. This device,

---

[1]Keith Ecker, "Making and Testing Brass Instruments," *The Instrumentalist*, October, 1960, p. 65.

[2]James Winter, *The Brass Instruments* (Boston: Allyn and Bacon, Inc., 1964), p. 49.

[3]*Ibid.*

however, has a tendency to result in poor intonation within the upper range of the bass trombone.

Selecting Trombone Players. A director who is not meticulous in the selection of his trombone students will usually be faced with a trombone section which is somewhat below his expectations. The trombone student should have above average general intelligence and a strong desire to play this instrument. In addition, he *must* possess excellent pitch discrimination. Since adjustment in pitch is accomplished by the slide, it is possible to play the trombone perfectly in tune. Conversely, if the student does not have a good ear, it is equally possible to play this instrument very much out of tune. Specific advantageous physical attributes include adequate arm length and lung capacity, a "square" jaw, a slightly receding lower jaw, and even front teeth.

The following recordings are recommended for use in teaching the trombone:

"Spotlight on Brass" (Voisin, Meek, and Orosz) VOX DL 300.

"Sonata for Trombone and Piano" by Hindemith. Roger Smith, Trombone. EMS 4.

Davis Shuman, Trombone—WQXR Strings. (Contemporary music for the trombone.) Golden Crest Record, #RE 7011.

John Swallow, Trombone and Harriet Wingreen, Piano. (Representative solo literature for trombone.) Golden Crest Record, #RE 7015.

Davis Shuman, Trombone. (Includes Rimsky-Korsakov *Concerto* and brass ensemble music.) Classic Edition #1041.

Caring for the Slide. The trombone should receive the same general care as any other brass instrument. The slide, however, is the most crucial component of the trombone in terms of care and maintenance. The inner slide is continually being exposed to the air while the trombone is being played. Therefore, this slide must be cleaned and oiled at frequent intervals by taking the outer slide off, wiping the inner slide with a lint-free soft cloth, and then applying several drops of high quality slide oil. Cold cream and water (applied with an atomizer) can be used in lieu of slide oil. Cold cream, however, should never be mixed with slide oil. A word of caution is advised against washing the slide with soap or detergent.

Any dent in the slide, even though very slight, should always be removed by a skilled repairman. Likewise, stuck mouthpieces and tuning slides that cannot be removed without force should be taken to a repairman. Considerable damage is often done to instruments when unqualified people attempt to do work that should be done by trained personnel. The student should be thoroughly familiar with the detailed instructions concerning the care of the trombone. These are readily available from any manufacturer of this instrument.

Teaching trombone playing

A good embouchure is essential in terms of achieving accurate pitch placement, a pleasing tone quality, and good intonation on the trombone. Generally, the basic trombone embouchure can be construed to be essentially the same as that used on the other low brass instruments. The "puckered" lip formation is favored by most authorities over the "semi-smile," or pulling back of the corners of the mouth. The actual placement of the mouthpiece on the lips tends to vary somewhat. Most trombonists prefer to play with more of the mouthpiece on the upper lip than on the lower lip. (See Figures 13-A and 13-B.)

Intrinsically intertwined with producing a pleasing and idiomatic tone on the trombone are such aspects as posture, breath support, embouchure, and *concept* of tone quality. By careful listening to his own tone quality and by analytical and critical listening to fine live performers, or performers on recordings, radio, and television, the student should gradually develop a full, rich and characteristic sound on his instrument.

Using Vibrato. Vibrato is generally accepted on the trombone and most players tend to prefer the "slide vibrato." This might be comparable to the hand vibrato on the trumpet or cornet. To produce this type of vibrato on the trombone, the slide is moved very slightly but rapidly to both the sharp and flat sides of the given notes. This vibrato is relatively easy to achieve. It should, however, be used with good taste and discretion at all times.

It is important to blow a steady stream of air through the trombone. The tongue should articulate (not interrupt) the flow of sound in a legato passage. A most common weakness in trombone tone quality (besides the lack of breath support) is the stuffy,

Figure 13–A   Trombone in Playing Position

nasal sound caused by playing with too little space between the
upper and lower teeth. The remedy is for the player to drop the
chin to a lower position in order to open the tone quality.

Using Alternate Slide Positions. Alternate positions on the trombone are made possible by this instrument's overtone series. They
are chiefly used in rapid, technical passages where the standard
slide positions would be impractical. These positions are also of
considerable value in making rapid and accurate adjustments in
intonation. Another valuable function of the alternate positions
is that they aid in the execution of slurs and slurred passages on
the trombone. The slurring problem on this instrument is unique

Figure 13–B   Trombone Embouchure

when compared to the other brass instruments. It has long been felt that a genuine slur on the trombone is only possible if the slide can be kept moving in the *opposite direction* of the notation involved in the slur. Since this is sometimes an impossibility the tongue needs to be employed to break the stream of air at precisely the same time that the slide is moved. Clearly, the stroke of the tongue for this purpose should be as light and imperceptible as possible.

Winter relates that there are 51 positions on the trombone.[4]

---

[4]James H. Winter, "Trombone Intonation," *National Association of College Wind and Percussion Instructors Bulletin*, Spring, 1966, p. 4.

These are, of course, modifications of the usual seven positions and are made possible by a number of discrepancies within the harmonic series. Indeed, instrument manufacturers attempt to raise the fifth harmonics to some extent by careful placement of constrictions or expansions in the taper of the instrument's tubing. This points up that the various positions on the trombone are not, in fact, fixed and unvaried locations on the slide of the instrument. The trombonist must depend on his ear in order to achieve good intonation. It is helpful for the trombone player to have at least a functional knowledge of the systems of intonation and the physics of his instrument.[5] There are, for example, four slide posi-

tions available for the high A♭.   Although third position is the one most commonly employed by trombonists, the first, fifth, and seventh may also be used. Whether or not an alternate slide position is used depends largely on the notation found in the passage involved; that is, what notes come before and what notes follow the note for which an alternate position might be advisable. A case in point is in passages such as the following: Within the context of this nota-

tional setting the D should not be played in the usual first position. Rather, it should be played in a "low fourth" position since it would be illogical to play the D in first position. Two other representative examples of alternate positions on the trombone are:

Possible: 1 6 1 2   1 6 1 2   3
Recommended: 6 —————————————————————————————

_____

[5]*Ibid.*, pp. 5–6.

Robert Getchell lists several useful alternate positions on the trombone:[6]

$+ =$ *Shorten position slightly*

$- =$ *Lengthen position slightly*

Much advanced solo, ensemble, and étude material employs the tenor and alto clefs as well as the bass clef. Although the tenor clef is more widely used than the alto clef, the student should gain reading facility in both.

A selected and annotated list of trombone solo literature for the development of specific individual skills

Bach-Beversdorf, Handel-Beversdorf, and Haydn-Beversdorf, *Endure! Endure!* (St. Matthew Passion), *Every Valley* (The Messiah), *And Now Revived He Springs* (The Seasons) (Southern Music Company). These are but three of a number of transcriptions by Beversdorf of arias by Bach, Handel, and Haydn. They are well within the capacities of high school trombonists and are particularly appropriate for presenting the various elements of baroque and classical music, reading in the tenor clef, and the development of a smooth, legato style on the trombone. The technical and musical difficulty of these arias places them on the moderately advanced level. Their accompaniments are also on this level of difficulty.

---

[6]Robert Getchell, *Teacher's Guide to the Brass Instruments* (Elkhart, Indiana: H. & A. Selmer Inc., 1959), p. 7.

Biber, *Sonata No. 3* (Musica Rara). This 17th century work is scored for trombone, two violins and continuo. The majority of the trombone part is written in the tenor clef and some rather wide skips are employed. Technically, this sonata is not greatly demanding and the trombone student should have ample opportunity to concentrate on tone quality, intonation, phrasing, and ensemble with the other instruments. All parts are on the moderately advanced level.

Clérisse-Voxman, *Prelude et Divertissement* (Rubank). This is an effective solo for the development of the moderately advanced trombone student. The opening section, "Prelude," contains sustained, legato passages as well as fluctuations in rhythm and mood. The "Divertissement" employs compound rhythm and requires a good technical command of the instrument. A clean, crisp staccato is also necessary in this section. The accompaniment is not difficult.

Creston, *Fantasy for Trombone and Orchestra* (G. Schirmer). This is a fine contemporary work for the advanced trombone student. Since it is generally regarded as one of the more difficult display pieces for the trombone, a technically advanced and musically mature trombonist is required. A number of rhythmic problems are present and the high range of the instrument is used extensively. The piano reduction is also on the advanced level.

Davison, *Sonata for Trombone and Piano* (Shawnee Press). This is a well-written contemporary sonata that should be appropriate for the development of the moderately advanced trombonist. It is scored in the bass clef and includes three movements. The first movement, "Fantasia," is quite lyrical in nature and employs a wide use of the instrument's relatively high register. The second movement, "After an English Folk-Song," should be particularly appropriate for the development of phrasing and breath control, and the rapid last movement demands considerable technical skill of the trombonist. Technically, the piano part would seem to be more demanding than the trombone part, and an advanced performer on this instrument is recommended.

Hartman (edited), *12 Trombone Solos* (G. Schirmer). *12 Trombone Solos* is a group of easy solos for the neophyte trombonist. The accompaniments are also on the easy level. Since the technical demands of the solos are quite nominal, the young trombonist should be able to concentrate on such aspects of performance as intonation, tone quality, phrasing, dynamics, and interpretation. This is a good "first" book of solo material.

Hindemith, *Sonata for Trombone and Piano* (Associated). Completed in 1941, this sonata was structured within the framework of a single movement. Within this movement, however, are many changes of mood and style. A wide range of the instrument is employed and the technical and rhythmic problems are considerable. Technically advanced and musically mature high school students should be able to profit from the study and performance of this work. The piano part is somewhat more demanding than the trombone part although both parts are clearly on the advanced level.

Hovhaness, *Concerto #3, "The Religious Singer,"* (Robert King Music Co.) This is a well-written contemporary English work for trombone (or baritone) and chamber orchestra. The solo part is especially idiomatically written for either of these instruments. The accompanying chamber orchestra consists of two violins, viola, cello, and string bass. Their parts are, for the most part, on the moderately advanced level of difficulty. Technically, the solo part is not too demanding and should be within the capacity of the moderately advanced trombone student.

Jacob, *Concerto for Trombone and Orchestra* (Mills). This contemporary Concerto for the trombone would require both a technically and musically advanced student. A very wide range of the instrument is utilized and the tenor clef is used extensively. While this work should prove challenging to the advanced high school trombone student, it should also be very valuable in the development of both his technical and musical competence on his instrument. The piano reduction is also on the advanced level and the orchestral accompaniment is available on rental.

Riviere, *Burlesque* (Leduc). *Burlesque* is an idiomatically written work on the moderately advanced level. Both bass and tenor clefs are used about equally. The opening "Grave" section will demand accuracy in rhythmical execution, and there are numerous quasi-diatonic passages that will require smooth, precise playing and accuracy in pitch placement. The accompaniment is also on the moderately advanced level.

Rousseau, *Piece Concertante* (Cundy-Bettoney). *Piece Concertante* is an effective work for the development of the moderately advanced high school trombonist. It is scored entirely in the bass clef and the notation lies well within the range of the instrument. Breath control, tone production, accurate pitch placement, phrasing, and rhythm are stressed in this solo. There is also a brief cadenza, and the closing section requires the use of a rapid tongue. The accompaniment is also on the moderately advanced level.

Roy, *Sonata for Trombone and Piano*, Opus 13 (Robert King). This contemporary sonata should prove to be both challenging and interesting to the mature high school trombonist and pianist. It is scored largely in the bass clef. The first movement, "Aria," is predominantly lyrical in nature and requires breath control, phrasing, and smooth legato playing. The second movement, "Interludio," has elements of jazz and demands a certain amount of technical skill on the instrument. The third movement, a passacaglia with 25 variations, is effectively and idiomatically written for the trombone. The piano part would appear to be somewhat more difficult than the trombone part, and an advanced pianist is recommended.

Smith, (edited) *Solos for the Trombone Player* (G. Schirmer). *Solos for the Trombone Player* contains several transcriptions as well as original works for the trombone. Technically, much of the material used in this book is not greatly demanding, thus providing opportunity for the student to concentrate on such important aspects of trombone performance as tone production, pitch placement, breath support, intonation, phrasing, and interpretation. Both solo parts and accompaniments range from the easy to the moderately difficult levels.

Strauss-Walters, *Allerseelen* (Rubank). This is an effective solo for the young trombonist. The technical requirements are not demanding and the key signature (3 flats) is common for this instrument. Thus the student should be able to concentrate on his tone quality, intonation, phrasing, and interpretation. The accompaniment is also on the easy level.

Voxman (edited), *Concert and Contest Collection for Trombone* (Rubank). This is a worthwhile collection. The levels of difficulty range from easy to moderately difficult. The solos found in this compilation are appropriate for use in the development of most facets of musical expression on the trombone, including rhythm, technical facility, tone production, extension of range, and interpretation. The accompaniments are also on the easy to moderately difficult levels.

Selected bibliography

Baines, Anthony (editor), *Musical Instruments Through The Ages.* London, England: Penguin Books Ltd., 1961.

Bate, Philip, *The Trumpet and Trombone.* New York, New York: W. W. Norton & Company, Inc., 1966.

Colin, Charles, *Vital Brass Notes*. Kenosha, Wisconsin: G. Leblanc Corporation, 1955.

Duerksen, George L., "The Voice of the Trombone," *The Instrumentalist*, vol. 19, October, 1964, p. 98.

Ecker, Keith, "Making and Testing Brass Instruments," *The Instrumentalist*, vol. 15, October, 1960, p. 64.

Farkas, Philip, *The Art of Brass Playing*. Bloomington, Indiana: Brass Publications, 1962.

Fink, Reginald H., "From Tenor to Bass Trombone," *The Instrumentalist*, vol. 16, January, 1962, p. 50.

Fink, Reginald H., "The Sound of a Bass Trombone," *The Instrumentalist*, vol. 16, June, 1962, p. 66.

Galpin, Francis W., *A Textbook of European Musical Instruments*. London, England: Ernest Benn Limited, 1937.

Geiringer, Karl, *Musical Instruments*. London, England: George Allen & Unwin Limited, 1943.

Getchell, Robert, *Teacher's Guide to the Brass Instruments*. Elkhart, Indiana: H. and A. Selmer Inc., 1959.

Graham, James, "Developing Your Bass Trombonists," *The Instrumentalists*, vol. 21, June, 1967, p. 49.

Graham, James, "The Legato Style of the Trombone," *The Instrumentalist*, vol. 19, May, 1965, p. 79.

Gray, Robert, "The Trombone in Contemporary Chamber Music," *Brass Quarterly*, vol. 1, September, 1957, p. 10.

Kleinhammer, Edward, *The Art of Trombone Playing*. Evanston, Illinois: Summy-Birchard Co., 1962.

Pottle, Ralph R., *Tuning the School Band and Orchestra*. Hammond, Louisiana: Ralph R. Pottle, 1960.

Rasmussen, Mary, *A Teacher's Guide to the Literature of Brass Instruments*. Durham, New Hampshire: *Brass Quarterly*, 1964.

Rasmussen, Mary, "A Bibliography of Choral Music with Trombone Ensemble Accompaniment, as compiled from Eleven Selected Sources," *Brass Quarterly*, vol. 5, Spring, 1962, p. 109.

Stauffer, Donald W., *Intonation Deficiencies of Wind Instruments in Ensemble*. Washington, D.C.: The Catholic University of America Press, 1954.

Tiede, Clayton H., *The Practical Band Instrument Repair Manual*. Dubuque, Iowa: Wm. C. Brown Co., 1962.

Winslow, Robert W. and John E. Green, *Playing and Teaching Brass Instruments*. Englewood Cliffs, New Jersey: Prentice-Hall, Inc., 1961.

Winter, James H., *The Brass Instruments*. Boston, Massachusetts: Allyn and Bacon, Inc., 1964.

Winter, James H., "Trombone Intonation," *National Association of College Wind and Percussion Instructors Bulletin*, vol. 14, Spring, 1966, p. 4.

Winter, James H., "Warm-up or Daily Calisthenics?" *National Association of College Wind and Percussion Instructors Bulletin*, vol. 16, Fall, 1967, p. 20.

CHAPTER 14

The Baritone

The baritone is an instrument truly indigenous to the band. Its origin can be traced into the mid 19th century. Some believe that there is a clear distinction between the baritone and the euphonium. Modern manufacturing techniques, however, make the difference minimal although the euphonium does have a somewhat larger bore. Both the baritone and euphonium are conically-bored instruments. When written in the bass clef the baritone is a non-transposing instrument. The treble clef baritone part is written a major ninth higher than the actual sound of the instrument. Clearly, the baritone is very important to the optimal functioning of the band. It is frequently referred to as "the cello of the band."

Selecting instructional materials

There is a paucity of instructional and solo literature written especially for the baritone. In terms of both instructional material and solo literature, the baritone student frequently uses trumpet, trombone, cello, and tuba literature. The following is intended to provide a representative listing to serve as a guide to the instrumental teacher.

Beginning Methods and Supplementary Studies

Foundation to Baritone Playing (Archimedes) .... Carl Fischer

Basic Method for the Baritone (Hindsley) .... Carl Fischer
Arban's Celebrated Method Part I
   (Ed. Randall-Mantia) .... Carl Fischer
Method for the Baritone, Book I (Beeler) .... Remick
Play Away! (Beeler) .... G. Schirmer
Elementary Method for Trombone or Baritone (Long) .... Rubank
Breeze-Easy Method for Baritone (Kinyon) .... Witmark

Intermediate Methods and Supplementary Studies

Method for the Baritone, Book II (Beeler) .... Remick
Daily Lip Drills and Studies for the Euphonium
   (Ronka) .... Carl Fischer
Lip Flexibility Exercises (W. M. Smith) .... Carl Fischer
Intermediate Method for Trombone or Baritone
   (Skornicka-Boltz) .... Rubank
60 Selected Studies for Bb Baritone, Book I
   (Kopprasch, Gumbert-Herbst) .... Carl Fischer
Arban's Celebrated Method Part II
   (Ed. Randall-Mantia) .... Carl Fischer
Daily Embouchure Studies (Goldman) .... Carl Fischer
Advanced Method for Trombone or Baritone
   (Gower-Voxman) .... Rubank
Selected Studies for Baritone (Voxman) .... Rubank
32 Melodies for Baritone (Vobaron) .... Carl Fischer

Advanced Methods and Supplementary Studies

60 Selected Studies for Bb Baritone, Book II
   (Kopprasch, Gumbert-Herbst) .... Carl Fischer
20 Melodic Studies or Caprices (Taylor) .... Fillmore
Professional's Key to Triple, Double, and Utility Tonguing
   (Schaefer) .... Fillmore
Odd Meter Etudes (Gates) .... Gornston
Melodious Etudes for Trombone (Bordogni-Rochut)
Volumes II and III .... Carl Fischer
15 Rhythmic Etudes (Bitsch) .... Leduc
26 Melodic Studies in Varied Rhythms and Keys
   (Blazhevich) .... Carl Fischer

Choosing a baritone, student adaptability, baritone recordings, and care of the baritone

The baritone is usually one of the most expensive instruments owned by the school system. The board of education (or individual purchasing the instrument) will actually save money over a period of time by purchasing a first-line instrument. Buying inexpensive instruments is usually a false sense of economy. The first-line baritone will generally be better in tune, perform in a superior fashion over a longer period of time, and require less repair work if given proper care.

Selecting a Good Baritone. Specifically, the baritone under consideration for purchase should have an easy response in blowing, good tone quality, and smooth, rapid valve action. It is also wise to purchase the four-valve model. The fourth valve extends the lower range of the instrument and also improves its intonation. A comparatively recent innovation is the addition of a small tuning slide attached to the baritone. This slide has a spring attachment which makes it possible for the player to correct faulty intonation immediately while playing. This device is very useful and worthy of consideration when purchasing a baritone. If possible, a brass specialist should check the instrument before the sale is finalized.

It is normally not wise to interchange trombone and baritone mouthpieces since the baritone mouthpiece should be both larger and deeper. Three widely used baritone mouthpieces are the H.N. White M-21, the Conn No. 2, and the Vincent Bach No. 11. The larger-bore euphonium requires a mouthpiece with a somewhat deeper cup and larger shank.

Since the baritone is essentially a solo instrument in the band, its player should possess adequate lung capacity and be a rather aggressive, extroverted performer. Clearly, the student should have an adequate degree of musical aptitude, a strong desire to play the instrument, good general intelligence, and the ability to persevere in the hard work which is required to develop his talent. Physically, a normal over-bite and straight, even front teeth are advantageous.

There is a scarcity of baritone recordings to aid in the instruction of the student when compared with the number of recordings available for most of the other band instruments. The following are suggested:

"Spotlight on Brass" (Voisin, Meek, and Orosz) VOX, DL 300.
"Euphonium Solos," Fred M. Dart, Euphonium. Coronet Program LP #1054. (Including: Haydn, *Adagio* (Cello Concerto),

Klengel: *Concertino No. I*, Guilmant, *Morceau Symphonique*, Bakaleinikoff, *Meditation*, Semler, *Barcarolle et Chanson Bachique*, Cords, *Concert Fantasie*, Takacs, *Sonata*, Rossini, *Largo al factotum*.)

"Leonard Falcone and His Baritone," Golden Crest Record #RE 7001. (Including: Clarke, *From the Shores of the Mighty Pacific*, Ponce, *Estrellita*, Bach, *Bourrèes I and II* from Suite #III (for cello), Simons, *Atlantic Zephyrs*, DeLuca, *Beautiful Colorado*, Ravel, *Piece en Forme de Habanera*, Senaille, *Allegro Spiritose*, Guilmant, *Morceau Symphonique*.)

"Leonard Falcone and His Baritone," Volume II. Golden Crest Record #RE 7016. (Including: Magnan, *Concerto*, Squire, *Tarantella*, Picchi-Mantia, *Fantasia Original*, Combelle, *Premier Solo de Concert*, Granados-Falcone, *Playera* (Danse Espagnole), Saint-Saëns, *Le Cygne* (The Swan), Pryor, *Blue Bells of Scotland*.

Caring for the Baritone. The baritone should receive the same general care as any other piston valve instrument. The valves should be cleaned frequently with warm water and then dried with cheesecloth. The valve casings should also be wiped dry. At least once a month the entire instrument should be flushed with *lukewarm*, soapy water. The bore can then be cleaned with a flexible wire bristle brush and the instrument rinsed (with cold tap water) and thoroughly drained.

Before the tuning slides and piston valves are replaced they should be greased and oiled respectively. The mouthpiece should also be cleaned and rinsed with a special mouthpiece brush or pipe cleaner. Cheesecloth can be used to clean and polish the exterior of the instrument if it is lacquered. Special lacquer cleaners and preservatives are available if desired. Music, books, and other articles should not be carried in the instrument's case. The student should be thoroughly familiar with the detailed instructions regarding the care of his instrument which are readily available from any manufacturer. Since baritones are usually school-owned, it is wise for the director to inspect frequently the condition of these instruments.

Teaching baritone playing

Winter refers to the embouchure as "the most probable source of the decline of the euphonium."[1] Contrary to some opinion, the

[1] James Winter, *The Brass Instruments*, p. 55.

baritone and trombone embouchures are not identical. Actually, the baritone embouchure should "utilize a definite inward-drawn pucker, not unlike the top of an old-fashioned lady's "poke" bag."[2] Many feel that the most advantageous position for the mouthpiece is in the center of the mouth with half of the mouthpiece on the upper lip and half on the lower lip. Some players prefer about two-thirds of the mouthpiece on the upper lip and one-third on the lower lip. Here again, it is probably unwise to indicate specific and rigid rules for all players to follow. Much depends on the physical make-up of the student's lips and mouth, as well as the beliefs and preferences of his instructor. (See Figures 14-A and 14-B.)

Figure 14–A   Baritone in Playing Position

[2]*Ibid.*

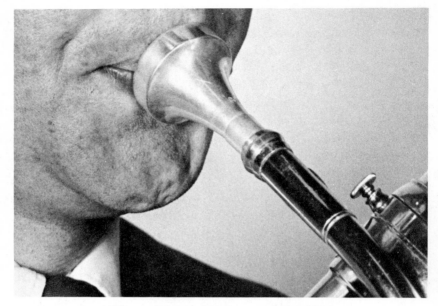

Figure 14–B   Baritone Embouchure

Excellent live performers and fine recordings should be very helpful in assisting the student to develop his concept of tone quality. Since the baritone offers little or no resistance in terms of consuming the player's wind, he must be especially careful in controlling the airstream into the instrument. In general terms, a lyrical tone that projects well and is pleasing to the ear should be sought.

Intonation on the baritone can be controlled by the following procedures:

1. The use of alternate fingerings. (This is especially possible with the four-valved instruments.)
2. Adjustment of the embouchure. (Major alterations of intonation are not normally possible or recommended through the method of embouchure adjustment.)
3. The use of the spring attachment mentioned previously.

In addition, compensating valves are now available on baritones and offer the following advantages:[3]

---

[3]Ralph R. Pottle, *Tuning the School Band and Orchestra* (Hammond, Louisiana: Ralph R. Pottle, 1962), p. 12.

1. They provide accurately tuned single valve tones.
2. Closer tuning on all valve combinations.
3. Superior tone quality because of reduced lipping.

The "lip" vibrato is probably the most widely used on the baritone. This is normally not difficult to accomplish since it involves only a *slight* raising and lowering of the jaw. This technique, of course, should be practiced slowly at first in order to acquire a *controlled* vibrato. As always, great care must be exercised by the player in order to make his vibrato musical and pleasing to the ear.

There is no question that every advanced baritone student should at least be able to read fluently in both the treble and bass clefs. Much of the better and more advanced étude and solo material is written in the bass clef. It is therefore particularly important that the student read in this clef fluently. Since the baritone utilizes a great deal of trombone and cello literature, it is also highly desirable that some fluency be achieved in the tenor clef as well.

A selected and annotated list of baritone solo literature for the development of specific individual skills

Bach-Kent, *Arioso* from Cantata #156 (Filmore). Although *Arioso* is not an especially strong solo for the development of technique on the baritone, it is most effective for the study of phrasing, tone production, intonation, and interpretation. It can also introduce the student to the baroque period of musical literature through one of the works of perhaps its greatest master. Both solo part and accompaniment are on the moderately difficult level.

The Baritone or Trombone Soloist (Carl Fischer). This compilation includes 37 well-known solos by such composers as Schubert, Rossini, Gounod, Chopin, and Mendelssohn. Technically, much of the material contained in this book is not greatly demanding, thus affording the student opportunity to concentrate on such vital aspects of baritone performance as interpretation, breath support, pitch placement, intonation, phrasing, and tone production. Both solo parts and accompaniments range from moderately easy to moderately difficult.

Boccalari, *Fantasia di Concerto* (Carl Fischer). *Fantasia di Concerto* is truly a display piece for the advanced baritone student. A great deal is required in terms of technical command of the instrument, recitative playing, breath support, and interpretation of numerous quasi-cadenza sections. This work should prove both challenging and interesting to the mature baritone student. Its accompaniment is technically less demanding than the solo part and a band accompaniment is available.

Brahms-Eckstein, *Cradle Song* (Carl Fischer). This is an effective first solo for the young baritone student. The middle range of the instrument is employed and only a nominal amount of technique is required. The accompaniment is also on the easy level.

Castleton, (trans.) *Nine Program Solos for Trombone* (Presser). This compilation includes transcriptions of works by Handel, Schumann, Bach, Mendelssohn, Mussorgsky, and others. It is a worthy contribution to the available solo literature for the secondary school trombone or baritone player. Technically, these solos are not too demanding and the player should be able to concentrate on such aspects of performance as intonation, tone quality, phrasing, dynamics, and interpretation. The solos and their accompaniments range from moderately easy to moderately difficult.

Clérisse-Voxman, *Prelude et Divertissement* (Rubank). This solo covers a farly wide range of the instrument in terms of both the low and high ranges. Although the key signature (three flats) is not a difficult one for the baritone, a number of rhythmic and technical problems are present. In general terms, *Prelude et Divertissement* is an effective solo for the development of rhythm and the treatment of specific rhythmic figures, legato and staccato tonguing, interpretation, and the extension of range. Both baritone and piano parts are on the moderately advanced level.

Gatti-Morra, *Concertino in Bb Major* (Carl Fischer). *Concertino* and its accompaniment are, for the most part, on the moderately difficult level. There are a number of changes of mood and style in this solo. Some sections require a rapid tongue while others stress a smooth, legato style. The notation lies within the baritone's range and, when performed well, it is an impressive solo.

Gumpert-Voxman, *Romanze* (Rubank). *Romanze*, as the title might imply, is essentially a melodic solo quite lyrical in nature. While technique as such is not stressed and the key (four flats) is a relatively common one for the baritone, a considerable amount of skill is required in the areas of breath support, tone production, and phrasing. Both baritone and piano parts are on the moderately advanced level of difficulty.

Kinyon (arr.), *Breeze-Easy Recital Pieces* (Witmark). This is a worthy compilation of beginning solos for the young baritone player. Most of the solos are well known and both accompaniments and solo parts are on the easy level. The works contained in this compilation should aid the student in the development and improvement of tone quality, breath support, intonation, phrasing, and interpretation.

Kryl, *King Carneval* (Carl Fischer). *King Carneval*, a concert polka, is somewhat of a display piece for the baritone. It was written by one of the best of the oldtime band leaders. A considerable amount of technical facility is required, and triple tonguing is also employed. Both the baritone part and its accompaniment are on the moderately difficult level. This solo is also available with band accompaniment.

Mullins, *Twelve Easy Classics for Trombone and Piano* (Summy-Birchard). This is a useful compilation of technically less difficult solos for the not-so-advanced secondary school trombone or baritone student. They make excellent material for the development of tone quality, phrasing, intonation, and interpretation. The solos and their accompaniments range from easy to moderately difficult.

Saint-Saëns-Trinkaus, *The Swan* (Fillmore). This is an effective adaptation to the baritone of Saint-Saëns' well-known work. Technically, the solo part is not demanding and is on the easy level. *The Swan* is an appropriate solo for the development of phrasing, tone control, breath support, and intonation. The accompaniment is somewhat more difficult than the solo part.

Simon, *Willow Echoes* (Fillmore). *Willow Echoes* is another effective and idiomatically written solo for the baritone by one of the famous band leaders of the professional band era. This solo contains numerous opportunities for the development of technique, phrasing, tone quality, and interpretation. The solo part is on the moderately difficult level and its accompaniment is somewhat less demanding.

Staigers, *Carnival of Venice* (Carl Fischer). This popular trumpet solo is, of course, a brilliant display piece which calls for an advanced performer with an unusually excellent technical command of his instrument. A great deal is required in the areas of tonguing, breath support, control, technique, and performing in the high range of the instrument. The accompaniment is less demanding than the solo part and a band accompaniment is available.

Voxman (edited), *Concert and Contest Collection for Baritone* (Rubank). This is a worthy compilation of solos for the secondary school baritone player. The technical and musical difficulty of these solos places them on the moderately easy to moderately difficult levels. They provide good material for the development of most aspects of musicianship on the baritone, including tone production, extension of range, rhythm, technical facility, legato and staccato tonguing, and interpretation. The accompaniments also range from moderately easy to moderately difficult.

Wagner-Trinkaus, *Song of the Evening Star* from Tannhäuser (Fillmore). This is an effective adaptation of Wagner's lovely melody to the baritone. Technically, the solo part is not difficult and the performer has opportunity to concentrate on such musical aspects of performance as beauty of tone, phrasing, intonation, and breath support. The solo part is on the moderately easy level. Technically, the accompaniment is somewhat more difficult.

Selected bibliography

Colin, Charles, *Vital Brass Notes*. Kenosha, Wisconsin: G. Leblanc Corporation, 1955.

Duvall, W. Clyde, *The High School Band Director's Handbook*. Englewood Cliffs, New Jersey: Prentice-Hall, Inc., 1960.

Eisenson, Jon, "Diaphragmatic Breathing," *Symphony*, vol. 5, March, 1951, p. 8.

Falcone, Leonard, "Baritone and Euphonium" in *Building Better Bands*. Rockville Centre, L.I., New York: Belwin, Inc., 1957.

Farkas, Philip, *The Art of Brass Playing*. Bloomington, Indiana: Brass Publications, 1962.

Geiringer, Karl, *Musical Instruments*. London, England: George Allen & Unwin Limited, 1943.

Getchell, Robert, *Teacher's Guide to the Brass Instruments*, Elkhart, Indiana: H. & A. Selmer Inc., 1959.

How to Care for Your Instrument. Elkhart, Indiana: C. G. Conn, Ltd., 1942.

Law, Glen C., "Development of Brass Tone," *The Instrumentalist*, vol. 15, November, 1960, p. 72.

Olsson, Phillip, "An Analytical Approach to Teaching Brass Instruments," *The School Musician*, vol. 39, October, 1967, p. 12.

Pottle, Ralph R., *Tuning the School Band and Orchestra*. Hammond, Louisiana: Ralph R. Pottle, 1960.

Rasmussen, Mary, *A Teacher's Guide to the Literature of Brass Instruments*. Durham, New Hampshire: *Brass Quarterly*, 1964.

Robbins, E. J., "So You Play the Euphonium?" *The Instrumentalist*, vol. 21, October, 1966, p. 63.

Stauffer, Donald W., *Intonation Deficiencies of Wind Instruments in Ensemble*. Washington, D.C.: The Catholic University of America Press, 1954.

Stauffer, Donald W., "The Master Tuner," (Part I) *The Instrumentalist*, vol. 17, May, 1963, p. 36.

Tiede, Clayton H., *The Practical Band Instrument Repair Manual*. Dubuque, Iowa: Wm. C. Brown Co., 1962.

Weast, Robert D., "The Development of Range," *The Instrumentalist*, vol. 16, November, 1961, p. 67.

Winslow, Robert W. and John E. Green, *Playing and Teaching Brass Instruments*. Englewood Cliffs, New Jersey: Prentice-Hall, Inc., 1961.

Winter, James H., *The Brass Instruments*. Boston, Mass.: Allyn and Bacon, Inc., 1964.

Young, Raymond G., "Euphonium—Well Sounding," *The Instrumentalist*, vol. 18, March, 1964, p. 72.

CHAPTER 15

The Tuba

The bass ophicleide, predecessor to the modern tuba, first appeared in Vienna during the early 19th century. About the middle of this century the first large BB*b* and CC basses were developed, and toward the end of the century the large basses used in the German bands of this period were becoming available. The first Sousaphone was manufactured in the United States in the early 20th century expressly for the famous Sousa Band. Most band tubas and Sousaphones today are the models in E*b* and BB*b*. Actually, both are essential to an effective tuba section.

A fine tuba section is a great asset to any band or wind ensemble. These instruments help to provide the foundation of the organization in terms of lyrical as well as rhythmical aspects of performance.

Selecting instructional materials

Both the quantity and quality of tuba instructional literature are somewhat lacking. This becomes particularly apparent on the higher levels of development. The more advanced tuba student frequently learns to transpose from literature written for the other brass instruments, such as the trumpet (transposed down two octaves) and the trombone (transposed down one octave). In addition, a certain amount of string (cello) and woodwind (bassoon) material can also be used to advantage by the tuba student. The following is a representative listing of instructional materials for the tuba.

Beginning Methods and Supplementary Studies
A Tune a Day for Tuba or Sousaphone
   (Herfurth-Miller) .... Boston
Method for Eb Tuba (Endreson) .... Cole
Method for BBb Tuba (Endreson) .... Cole
Method for the Tuba, Volume I (Beeler) .... Remick
Play Away! (Beeler) .... G. Schirmer
Basic Method for Tuba (Hindsley) .... Carl Fischer
Tutor for Eb Bass (Langey) .... Carl Fischer
Foundation to Tuba and Sousaphone Playing
   (Bell) .... Carl Fischer
Elementary Method for Eb or BBb Bass (Hovey) .... Rubank
Breeze-Easy Method for Tuba (Kinyon) .... Witmark
First Book of Practical Studies for the Tuba
   (Getchell-Hovey) .... Belwin

Intermediate Methods and Supplementary Studies
Intermediate Method for Eb or BBb Bass
   (Skornicka-Boltz) .... Rubank
Method for Tuba (Geib) .... Carl Fischer
Second Book of Practical Studies for Tuba
   (Getchell-Hovey) .... Belwin
Method for the Tuba, Volume II (Beeler) .... Remick
Advanced Method for Eb or BBb Bass, Volume I
   (Gower-Voxman) .... Rubank
Studies and Lip Drills for Tuba (Ronka) .... Carl Fischer
Outlines of Technic, Parts I and 2 (Prescott) .... Carl Fischer

Advanced Methods and Supplementary Studies
66 Etudes in All Major and Minor Keys (Slama) .... Carl Fischer
70 BBb Tuba Studies
   (Blazhevich) .... State Music Publishers, Moscow
Advanced Method for the Eb or BBb Bass, Volume II
   (Gower-Voxman) .... Rubank
Melodious Etudes for Trombone, Volumes II and III
   (Bordogni-Rochut) .... Carl Fischer
15 Rhythmic Etudes (Bitsch) .... Leduc
26 Melodic Studies in Varied Rhythms and Keys
   (Blazhevich) .... Carl Fischer

Choosing a tuba, student adaptability, tuba recordings,
and care of the tuba

Probably the most common basses found in American bands
today are the Sousaphone, the upright bass, and the so-called
recording bass. (See Figure 15-A.) Under ideal conditions many
believe that *both* the upright bass and the recording bass should
be used in the concert band. It is also advisable to use one E*b*
bass in the band. The E*b* bass, doubling the usual BB*b* tubas one
octave higher wherever possible, has a tendency to clear up passages lying in the low register of the BB*b* tuba.[1] Clearly, the upright bass or recording model is best for solo and ensemble work.
In cases where only a limited amount of money is available for
instruments, however, the Sousaphone is probably the most practical model since it can serve both concert and marching organizations.

Tubas are among the most expensive instruments normally purchased by the school system. Yet, money can be saved by securing
first-line instruments. The least expensive tubas usually present
many problems in terms of intonation, tone quality, and general
mechanical construction which can lead to numerous repair bills.
The tuba, like many similar brass instruments, should have good
tone quality, smooth, rapid valve action, and an easy response
in blowing. Models are also available with four valves and a
compensating device which lowers the range and improves the
intonation of the instrument. These features merit the consideration of the director as he selects the tubas for his band. If he is
not a brass specialist it would be wise for him to solicit the services of such a person to inspect the instruments before they are
purchased.

Selecting Tuba Players. Since the tuba is a rather large instrument it is essential that the student have adequate lung capacity
for this instrument. On the other hand, the size of the student
per se should certainly not be the only factor, or even the deciding
one, in selecting students for the tuba. The student should have
a strong desire to play the instrument, good general intelligence,
an adequate degree of musical aptitude, and the ability to follow

[1]Gerald C. Meyer, "The Tuba Section," *The Instrumentalist*, December, 1960,
p. 57.

Figure 15–A   Recording Bass in Playing Position

through with regular and diligent practice. Physically, straight and even front teeth and rather heavy lips are advantageous.

There is not a large number of solo tuba recordings available to use as instructional aids. The following are recommended:

"Spotlight on Brass" (Voisin, Meek, and Orosz) VOX DL 300.

"Tuba Solos," Rex Conner, Tuba. Coronet Program LP #1259.

Harvey Phillips, Tuba. Golden Crest Record #7006.

William Bell, Tuba. Golden Crest Record #3015.

Peter Popiel, Tuba and Henry Fuchs, Piano. Mark Educational Recording #MRS 28437.

Care of the Tuba. The tuba should receive the same general care as recommended for the other brass instruments in general and the brass piston valve instruments in particular. Since the tubas and/or Sousaphones are usually school-owned, it is suggested that they be frequently inspected by the band director. They seem to be especially susceptible to dents and the accumulation of various items which apparently enter these instruments through their large bells. This, of course, can have a deleterious effect on the intonation, tone quality, and overall mechanical functioning of the instruments. It is also wise to have *all* school-owned instruments inspected once a year by a skilled instrument repair specialist. Adequate locker facilities should be available for all band instruments, both privately-owned and school-owned. In addition, cases should be provided for all school-owned instruments. This is especially important if the band goes on tour or travels to out-of-town athletic events, parades and the like. Since both tubas and Sousaphones are readily noticeable to audiences, it is essential that these instruments be well polished for all public appearances. The student should have enough personal pride in his instrument to keep it in good mechanical condition and looking well at all times. Detailed instructions regarding care and maintenance are readily available from any manufacturer.

Teaching tuba playing

All three forms of the band tuba (the Sousaphone, the upright bass, and the recording bass) are available in various bore sizes ranging from a relative small bore to a very large bore. Generally, an instrument with a medium bore is the best choice. The small-bore instrument is usually not able to produce the big idiomatic sound normally characteristic of the tuba. On the other hand, the excessively large-bored tuba is very taxing on the player's wind supply and also tends to produce a rather heavy and somewhat unclear tone.

A medium-sized mouthpiece is also recommended since an overly large mouthpiece does not serve to enhance the instrument's tone quality. A great deal of latitude is available to the tuba player in terms of mouthpiece placement. This is due to the comparatively large size of even a medium-sized tuba mouthpiece. Farkas, however, points out that:

> This does not imply that the tuba player can carelessly place the mouthpiece anywhere on his lips. The "ideal spot" produces such superior results in all phases of playing that the tuba player is well justified in spending some experimental time seeking it.[2]

Pressure is normally not a problem with most tuba players. The large mouthpiece permits both lips to vibrate freely and, much of the time, this instrument plays in a relatively low register. In terms of selecting a tuba mouthpiece, Winter recommends those produced by the H.N. White Co., the Vincent Bach Co., and the "Revelation" series of the Holton Co.[3]

Developing a Concept of Tuba Tone. Excellent live performers as well as fine recordings can be useful in helping the tuba student to develop a tonal concept. This is particularly important on the tuba since many high school players woefully lack the lightness and finesse so essential to fine tuba playing in both solo and ensemble performance. A lyrical tone quality that has a degree of firmness with good control should be sought. It is also essential that the student control his air-supply since the instrument itself offers virtually no resistance.

Proper Tuba Embouchure. A most common weakness of tuba tone quality is caused by faulty embouchure formation, such as puffed cheeks and embouchures that are too relaxed. In addition, many players simply do not blow enough air through the instru-

---

[2]Philip Farkas, *The Art of Brass Playing* (Bloomington, Indiana: Brass Publications, 1962), p. 34.

[3]James Winter, *The Brass Instruments*, p. 59.

ment to produce a good, idiomatic tone. The facial muscles should hold the embouchure firmly against the teeth and facial bones. Actually, a flat and somewhat pointed chin is an essential characteristic of good embouchure formation on all brass instruments. The chin should never be rounded as in a poor clarinet embouchure. (See Figure 15-B.)

THIS   NOT THIS

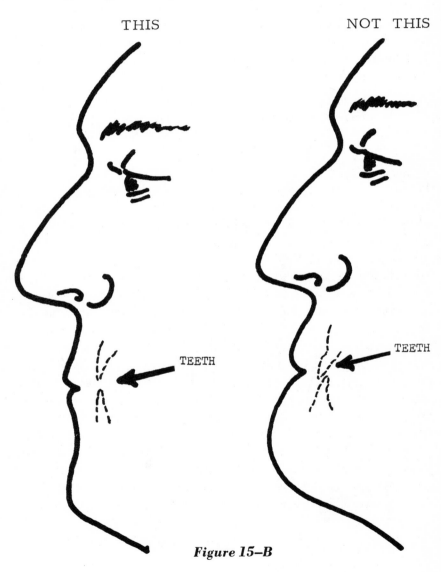

Figure 15–B

There should be more space between the upper and lower teeth on the tuba than on the trombone. If there is too little space the tone quality will have a tendency to be somewhat stuffy (on *piano* levels) and somewhat nasal (on *forte* levels). The chin should be quite low in the tuba embouchure. (See Figure 15-C.)

Intonation on the tuba can, to some extent, be controlled by the embouchure. Better ways of controlling intonation involve the use of alternate valve combinations, the use of tubas which have four valves, and the built-in compensating device. Clearly, the four-valve tuba makes many more valve combinations available to the player. The finest equipment, however, is no substitute for the student having good pitch discrimination and being taught (from his earliest lessons) to constantly *listen* to his tone quality and accuracy of intonation.

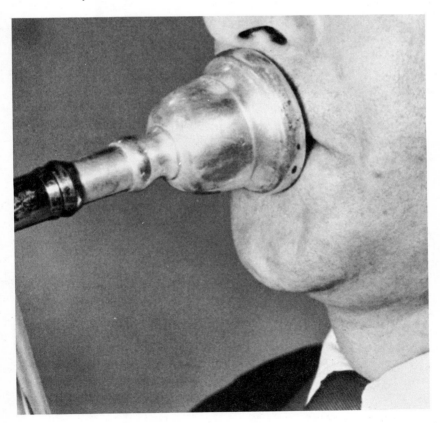

Figure 15–C   Bass Embouchure

The following notes tend to be either sharp or flat as indicated
by + (sharp) and — (flat).

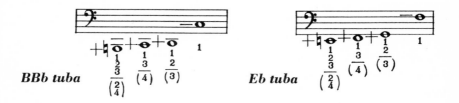

BBb tuba   **Eb tuba**

The majority of tuba manufacturers now correct the flatness by
shortening the first valve slide. The sharpness can be corrected
by pulling out the first valve slide. If a fourth valve is included
on the tuba the recommended fingerings in parenthesis should
be employed.[4] The first valve slide is the slide most frequently
used in pitch adjustment on the tuba. Bell epitomizes the tuba
intonation problem in the following manner: "The most important thing to look for when buying a tuba is to find one on which
the open tones are in tune." He continues: "Having found an
instrument with good open tones and one on which the first, third,
and fourth valve slides can be manipulated with the left hand,
there should be no excuse for playing any note out of tune."[5]

Vibrato and Tonguing on the Tuba. Vibrato is rarely employed
in band tuba literature and normally should not be used unless
the conductor requests it. Due to the size of the instrument, the
"lip" vibrato is most widely accepted on the tuba. This technique
involves a *slight* raising and lowering of the jaw and should be
practiced slowly at first. The achievement of a good basic tone is
very much a prerequisite to the development of vibrato. Great
care must be taken by the player to make his vibrato musical and
pleasing to the ear.

A clean, firm but relatively light attack should be used when
tonguing on the tuba. Too often the high school tuba student
seems to develop a heavy, pointed, and often harsh tonguing
technique which tends to distort both the pitch and tone quality.

---

[4]William J. Bell, *A Handbook of Information on Intonation* (Elkhorn, Wisconsin: The Getzen Company, Inc., 1965), p. 1.
    [5]*Ibid.*

The multiple-tonguings (see Chapter 13, "The Trumpet") are not widely used on the tuba. Nevertheless, the tuba student should become acquainted with these techniques.

A selected and annotated list of tuba solo literature for the development of specific individual skills

Beversdorf, *Sonata for Tuba and Piano* (Interlochen). Completed in 1956, this *Sonata* is generally believed to be one of the finest of the contemporary sonatas for the tuba. An advanced technician and mature musician is required for the performance of this three-movement work. Although the composer generally avoids the high register of the tuba, a great deal is required in terms of breath control, technique, and musicianship. The piano part is also on the advanced level.

Hartley, *Sonatina for Tuba and Piano* (Interlochen). This contemporary *Sonatina* was completed in 1961 and is comprised of three relatively brief movements. The composer utilizes the best playing range of the instrument throughout the composition. Technically, it is not unduly difficult, and the player should be able to concentrate on such important aspects of performance as tone quality, intonation, breath support, tonguing, and interpretation. The tuba and piano parts are generally on the moderately difficult level.

Hindemith, *Sonata for Tuba and Piano* (Associated). Published in 1957, many feel this work is the finest contemporary sonata for the tuba. This *Sonata* presents the player with a number of problems in terms of many wide skips of notation (such as ninths, elevenths, and sevenths), changes of meter, and quasi-recitative playing. It should be both challenging and rewarding to the advanced tuba student. An advanced pianist is also required.

Kinyon (arr.), *Breeze-Easy Recital Pieces for Tuba* (Witmark). Most of the solos found in this compilation are well known and their accompaniments are generally quite easy. This is a fine first book of solos for the neophyte tuba student of any age. Another book which falls into this same category is the *Soloist Folio for Tuba* (arr.) published by Rubank. The solos found in these books can be used to good advantage for the development of most aspects of musicianship on the tuba including breath support, tone production, control of pitch, phrasing, and interpretation.

Kreisler, *Allegretto Grazioso* (Southern). *Allegretto Grazioso* is comprised of two movements. It is especially well suited to the secondary school tuba student who does not have a great amount of experience on the instrument. Its demands, in terms of range and technique, are modest and this work should provide good material for either contest or recital. Both tuba and piano parts are on the moderately easy level of difficulty.

Mueller, *Concert Music for Bass Tuba* (Interlochen). This work was completed in 1946 and is dedicated to Arnold Jacobs of the Chicago Symphony Orchestra. Although some chordal dissonances are present, the rhythm is fairly straightforward with no tempo or meter changes. Other than a brief middle section, this solo is not difficult technically. It is a particularly good solo for the study and development of tone quality. Both solo part and accompaniment are on the moderately difficult level.

Nelhybel, *Suite for Tuba and Piano* (Boston). This *Suite*, published in 1966, is comprised of five movements entitled: "Allegro marcato," "Quasi improvisando," "Allegretto," "Slow," and "Allegro con bravuta." The majority of the notation is well within the comfortable playing range of the instrument. A number of rhythmic problems are present and there are some meter changes in the third movement. In general, this is a very idiomatically written work that should be of interest to the moderately advanced tuba student. The piano part is also on the moderately advanced level.

Painpare-Voxman, *Concertpiece* (Rubank). This solo should provide the less-advanced tuba student with the opportunity to develop his staccato tonguing, phrasing, and technique. Several small intervallic skips are prevalent in the notation and there is a brief opening cadenza. The key (three flats) is an elementary one for the tuba. The solo part is generally on the moderately easy level as is its accompaniment.

Persichetti, *Seranade #12 for Solo Tuba* (Elkan-Vogel). This unaccompanied *Seranade* was commissioned by the professional tuba player Harvey Phillips and was published in 1963. It clearly requires a mature tuba student for performance. A very wide range is utilized by the composer and a considerable amount of technical proficiency is demanded. This work includes six movements, all of which are comparatively brief.

Schmidt, *Serenade for Tuba and Piano* (Avant). Published in 1962, this *Serenade* includes four movements entitled: *Romanza, Waltz, Dirge,* and *March.* This composition is an especially interesting solo for the moderately advanced to advanced secondary school tuba student. All four movements are idiomatically written and, for the most part, a moderate playing range of the instrument is used. There are some rather difficult technical passages but technique, per se, should not prove to be a prohibiting factor. The piano part tends to be on the advanced level.

Telemann-Chidester, *Prelude and Allegretto* (Southern). These two movements have been transcribed and arranged for tuba and piano from two well-known sonatas by Telemann. Both movements are relatively brief. The *Prelude* (Adagio) is especially appropriate for the development of the lower range of the instrument and the study of tone production in this register. The *Allegretto* (Tempo di Minuetto) presents few technical difficulties and the student should be free to concentrate on dynamic control, pitch placement, and phrasing. The tuba part is on the moderately easy level and the piano part is somewhat more difficult.

Vandercook, *Colossus* (Rubank). *Colossus* is written in the form of theme and variations. The rhythms are straightforward and the key signature (three flats) is a common one for the tuba. Most of the notation lies within a comfortable playing range of the instrument. This solo should be especially appropriate for the development of technique, articulation, and the treatment of various rhythmic figures. Both the solo part and accompaniment are on the moderately easy level.

Voxman (edited), *Concert and Contest Collection for Eb or BBb Bass (Tuba) and Piano* (Rubank). This is a fine collection for the secondary school tuba student. The technical and musical difficulty of the solos found in this book is on the moderately easy to moderately difficult levels. These solos can be used to advantage in the development of most aspects of musicianship on the tuba, including the extension of range, development of rhythm, technique, tonguing, tone production, and interpretation. The accompaniments also range from moderately easy to moderately difficult.

Wekselblatt (edited), *Solos for the Tuba Player* (G. Schirmer). *Solos for the Tuba Player* contains adaptations of works by such composers as Wagner, Berlioz, Bernstein, Mozart, and others. Technically, much of the material used in this book is not too demanding, thus making it possible for the student to concentrate on such important aspects of performance as tone production, breath support, intonation, and phrasing. Both solo parts and accompaniments range from the easy to moderately difficult levels.

Selected bibliography

Baines, Anthony (editor), *Musical Instruments Through The Ages.* London, England: Penguin Books Ltd., 1961.

Bell, William J., *A Handbook of Information on Intonation.* Elkhorn, Wisconsin: The Getzen Company, Inc., 1965.

Colin, Charles, *Vital Brass Notes.* Kenosha, Wisconsin: G. Leblanc Corporation, 1955.

Conner, Rex A., "Discussing the Tuba," *The Instrumentalist*, vol. 19, December, 1964, p. 80.

Conner, Rex A., "Tuba Talk," *The Instrumentalist*, vol. 16, October, 1961, p. 49.

Duvall, W. Clyde, *The High School Band Director's Handbook.* Englewood Cliffs, New Jersey: Prentice-Hall, Inc., 1960.

Eisenson, Jon, "Diaphragmatic Breathing," *Symphony*, vol. 5, March, 1951, p. 8.

Farkas, Philip, *The Art of Brass Playing.* Bloomington, Indiana: Brass Publications, 1962.

Getchell, Robert, *Teacher's Guide to the Brass Instruments*, Elkhart, Indiana: H. & A. Selmer Inc., 1959.

How to Care for Your Instrument. Elkhart, Indiana: C. G. Conn, Ltd., 1942.

Kuehn, David L., "A Selected List of Tuba Literature," *The Instrumentalist*, vol. 17, December, 1962, p. 48.

Marzan, Fred J., "Twentieth Century Literature for the Tuba," Morehead State University, 1967. (Mimeographed.)

Meyer, Gerald C., "The Tuba Section," *The Instrumentalist*, vol. 15, December, 1960, p. 57.

McMillen, Hugh, "Tuba" in *Building Better Bands.* Rockville Centre, L.I., New York: Belwin, Inc., 1957.

Pottle, Ralph R., *Tuning the School Band and Orchestra.* Hammond, Louisiana: Ralph R. Pottle, 1960.

Rasmussen, Mary, *A Teacher's Guide to the Literature of Brass Instruments.* Durham, New Hampshire: *Brass Quarterly*, 1964.

Smith, Leonard B., "Controlled Breathing," *The Instrumentalist*, vol. 11, September, 1956, p. 83.

Stauffer, Donald W., *Intonation Deficiencies of Wind Instruments in Ensemble.* Washington, D.C.: The Catholic University of America Press, 1954.

Stauffer, Donald W., "The Master Tuner," (Part I) *The Instrumentalist*, vol. 17, May, 1963, p. 36.

Tetzlaff, Daniel, "Enemies of Endurance," *International Musician*, vol. 54, December, 1955, p. 24.

Tetzlaff, Daniel, "Let's Stress Fundamentals," *The Instrumentalist*, vol. 10, March, 1956, p. 48.

Tiede, Clayton H., *The Practical Band Instrument Repair Manual*. Dubuque, Iowa: Wm. C. Brown Co., 1962.

Winslow, Robert W. and John E. Green, *Playing and Teaching Brass Instruments*. Englewood Cliffs, New Jersey: Prentice-Hall, Inc., 1961.

Winter, James H., *The Brass Instruments*. Boston, Mass.: Allyn and Bacon, Inc., 1964.

IV

TEACHING THE PERCUSSION FOR INDIVIDUAL SKILLS

CHAPTER 16

The Snare Drum

It is a generally accepted fact that the first musical instruments used by man were crude predecessors of the percussion family. Within the context of our present culture, however, the percussion instruments are probably the last group to be developed and used to their full potential. Such contemporary composers as Orff, Stravinski, Bartók, and Ives have required the percussion instruments to play major roles in many of their compositions. There is also an increasing amount of fine literature being written for the modern percussion ensemble.

The rapid and constant improvement of the percussion instruments has also been a significant factor in the acceptance of this family as a truly *musical* group of instruments. The many excellent percussion ensembles found in all parts of the United States further attest to the rapid strides this group of instruments has made. Few would debate the vital role a percussion section assumes within the modern concert band.

Selecting instructional materials

To parallel the growth and acceptance of the percussion family one finds an abundance of excellent instructional materials for the percussion instruments in general and for the snare drum in particular. The following is a representative compilation which might serve as a guide to the instructor.

197

Beginning Methods and Supplementary Studies

Basic Method for the Drums (Berryman) .... Carl Fischer
Drum Method, Book I (Harr) .... Cole
Fundamental Approach to the Snare Drum (Parks) .... Sam Fox
Elementary Method for Drums (Yoder) .... Rubank
Progressive Studies for the Snare Drum, Book I
    (Gardner) .... Carl Fischer
Modern Method, Part 1, (Gardner) .... Carl Fischer
Beginning Snare Drum Method (Price) .... Morris
Three R's for Snare Drum—Reading, Rhythms, Rudiments,
    Book I (Ostling) .... Belwin

Intermediate Methods and Supplementary Studies

Drum Method, Book II (Harr) .... Cole
Rolls, Rolls, Rolls, (Rothman) .... J. R. Publications
The Art of Drumming (Moore) .... Ludwig
Progressive Studies for the Snare Drum, Book II
    (Gardner) .... Carl Fischer
Three R's for Snare Drum—Reading, Rhythms, Rudiments,
    Book II (Ostling) .... Belwin
Intermediate Method for Drums (Buggert) .... Rubank
The Drummer's Heritage (Fennell) .... Carl Fischer
Practical Method of Developing Finger Control
    (Burns-Malin) .... Henry Adler
Variations of Drumming (Pace) .... Drum Book Music

Advanced Methods and Supplementary Studies

The Solo Drummer (Harris) .... G. Ricordi
Cadences for All Occasions (Schinstine) .... Southern
Advanced Method for Drums (Whistler) .... Rubank
Progressive Studies for the Snare Drum, Books 3 and 4
    (Gardner) .... Carl Fischer
Latin-American Rhythms for the Drummer (Rale) .... Remick
The Art of the Tympanist and Drummer
    (Shivas) .... Dobson (London)
Latin American Rhythm Instruments (Majales & Adler) .... Adler

Choosing the drum, student adaptability, representative recordings, and care of the drum

Bartlett lists over 60 different instruments in his system of classification for percussion instruments.[1] This comprehensive listing

---

[1]Harry R. Bartlett, *Guide to Teaching Percussion* (Dubuque, Iowa: Wm. C. Brown Company, 1964), pp. 9–10.

includes both the standard instruments as well as the somewhat esoteric members of the percussion family. The present discussion will necessarily be concerned with the principal percussion instruments normally associated with the high school band; that is, the snare drum, base drum, cymbals, timpani, and the mallet instruments. This chapter will, of course, deal with the snare drum.

Probably the most widely used concert band snare drums are the models with dimensions of 5 inches, 6½ inches, or 8 inches in depth and 14 inches in diameter. The depth of the drum tends to have a significant effect on its tone color; for example, a shallower drum will produce a *brighter* sound, whereas the deeper drum will produce a *darker* sound. The field drum is, of course, a larger instrument with a 15 or 16 inch diameter and a depth of 10 or 12 inches. Plastic drumheads are increasingly replacing the traditional calfskin head in most high school bands. Drums with wood shells and wire snares are also recommended. The 5B and 2B drum sticks have proved quite acceptable for concert performance, while the 1S and 2S sticks seem to achieve the best results with the marching band.

Probably the most important single factor in selecting percussion students is that of *rhythm.* All percussionists should possess an outstanding sense of rhythm. Good general intelligence and enthusiasm are also important, and a piano background is helpful. Innate musical talent and fine pitch sensitivity are essential. Physically, the student should have better-than-average wrist dexterity and flexibility. It is usually expected that percussion students will learn to perform on a number of the many percussion instruments, and every serious percussion student should acquire some depth on all of the principal percussion instruments.

There are a number of recordings available for use as instructional aids in the development of the percussion student. The following are representative:

"The 26 Standard American Drum Rudiments and Selected Solos," Frank Arsenault, Percussionist. Available from Ludwig Drum Co.

Percussion (2-record set) explained in words and sound. Saul Goodman, Percussionist. Capitol album No. HBR 21003.

"Ruffles and Flourishes," Eastman Symphonic Wind Ensemble, Frederick Fennell, conductor. Mercury record #50112.

"Percussion Music," Saul (Sandy) Feldstein, Percussionist. Golden Crest record #CR-1005.

"American Percussion Society," Paul Price, conductor. Urania record #UX-106.

The percussion family is perhaps the easiest group of musical instruments to care for and maintain. Their overall construction is relatively simple when compared with some of the other musical instruments. One of the best ways to insure proper care for the percussion instruments is to provide adequate storage cabinets for them. Portable cabinets, which can be moved to and from the rehearsal location with ease, are quite popular among band directors. It is wise to control both the temperature and humidity in the storage cabinets or areas. A temperature of about 70 degrees Fahrenheit with approximately 45 per cent humidity should be maintained.

Sticks are frequently either lost or broken, and a supply should be kept on hand at all times. The "membrane" percussion instruments require more care than the others. Broken or cracked plastic heads are easily replaced, and several new heads should be immediately available when the need arises. Various commercial materials are normally used to clean and polish the percussion instruments. These include: brass polish for cymbals, furniture polish for wood shells, and chrome cleaner for the metal drum fittings. Many directors use an art gum eraser to clean drumheads. The plastic drum shells can be washed and then waxed for better appearance.

Since most percussion instruments are school-owned, it is wise for the director to make periodic inspections. The students should become familiar with instructions regarding the care and maintenance of the instrument they play. These are readily available from any percussion manufacturer.

Teaching snare drum

The hand positions for the snare drum might be described as follows:

A. Right Hand Position

The right stick should be held between the thumb and the second joint of the forefinger with the remaining

Figure 16–A   Snare Drum, Preparatory Position

three fingers curling around the stick. The thumb should
be placed on the stick as though it were a part of it. As
the stick strikes the drum, the top of the hand should be
visible. (See Figure 16-A.)

B. Left Hand Position

The left stick should be gripped in the socket between

Figure 16–B   Snare Drum, Playing Position

the thumb and first finger. The fourth and the little
fingers then curl around the stick at the second joint, thus
allowing the stick to rest there. The first finger should
curve over the stick with the thumb resting on it, while
the middle finger should curve slightly, thus serving as a
directional guide for the stick. (See Figure 16-B.)

Bartlett includes the following common faults in the right and
left handholds:

Stick not held at balancing point (1/3 distance from butt end).

R thumb pointing down instead of straight along shaft.

Forming R grip with second instead of index finger.

R wrist not flat but tilted over to the right.

L wrist not vertical but tilted over to the left.

L stick not held firmly enough at fulcrum.

Index and second fingers of L hand pressing down on stick shaft.

L wrist bent out away from body instead of extending straight from forearm.[2]

For the "like hand manner" position both sticks should be held in the right hand position. They should be held tight enough so that they will not fall out of the player's hands, and yet loose enough to achieve the proper bounce. After the student gets the proper feel of the sticks he should be instructed in playing the stroke and rebound:

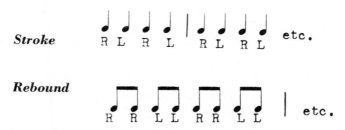

Stroke   R L R L | R L R L   etc.

Rebound   R R L L R R L L | etc.

The proper height, alternation, and evenness of the sticks should be stressed. The student should become familiar with note values and their subdivisions. He should work a great deal on the roll, the ruff, and the flam, since all 26 of the basic drum rudiments are essentially variations of these. In the course of his study the drummer should be instructed in sightsinging and basic music theory. He should be made aware of the various elements of musical interpretation; such as, dynamics, tone quality, tempo, rhythm and the like. After the player has achieved an adequate playing and reading technique, he should read as much drum material as possible. This material should include literature from all periods. As he becomes more advanced, the drummer should seek to gain some facility on a number of the other percussion instruments.

How to Roll. Rolls are generally considered the most vital rudi-

---

[2]*Ibid.*, p. 30.

ment of percussion playing, and they frequently afford the drummer with his biggest single obstacle. There are a number of rolls that must be learned as an integral part of the percussionist's basic knowledge and skills.

The open double stroke roll, sometimes referred to as the "mama-daddy" roll, is essentially the basis for the study and development of all other rolls. This roll is executed by two clear bounces from each of the sticks. It is mandatory that the drummer learn to control the open double stroke roll at different speeds, for in so doing he will be able to execute *with control* any of the other rolls. Clearly, a great deal of slow, meticulous practice is required to develop this roll. After the open double stroke roll has been mastered, the "press roll" can be achieved by the player literally pressing the stick a bit more into the drumhead. The press roll is employed mostly in dance work and concerts, whereas the open double stroke roll is found largely in contest literature and marches.

With the exception of the tympani, the only way a drummer can execute a sustained note is through the process of rolling. The practice of rolls is perhaps the best way for the student to develop the high degree of control required of a percussion player. Some teachers advocate allotting as much as 60 to 70 per cent of the student's practice time to the practice and perfecting of rolls.

Bartlett lists the following common faults for the long roll:

> Failure to maintain an even rate of acceleration in passing over the "break" (traditional approach). Making more than one bounce sound following each tap (newer approach).
>
> Failure to make the bounce equal to the tap. Gaps in the long roll due to poor timing of wrist alterations.
>
> Pressing or crushing sticks down into drumhead, resulting in scratchy texture of roll.
>
> Stiffness of wrist action.[3]

Correct sticking should play an important role in drumming. A fundamental rule of good snare drumming indicates that, as much as possible, the same sticking should be used for identical meas-

---

[3]*Ibid.*, p. 45.

ures with the right hand normally leading. This is illustrated in Figure 16-C.

Figure 16–C

The desired goal is, of course, to make each measure and/or rhythmical pattern sound the same. Conversely, if different stickings are used for each figure they will not sound the same to the trained ear. This occurs because two different drum sticks are being used, the drummer's right and left hands are not usually evenly developed, and the drum is being hit on two different areas.

Other basic rules for good sticking are:

1. Start with the right hand and alternate in the case of two or more eighth notes in a series.
2. Start with the right hand and alternate when there are two or more sixteenth notes in a series.
3. Eighth notes which fall on up-beats should usually be played with the left hand.

Common stickings for flams and ruffs are shown in Figures 16-D, 16-E, and 16-F.

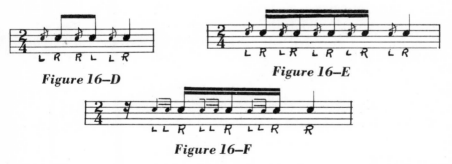

Figure 16–D

Figure 16–E

Figure 16–F

Starting and ending all rolls with the right hand helps to achieve a uniformity of sound. Time signatures such as 12/8, 3/4, and 9/8 require a deviation from the rule of starting each measure with the right hand since the left hand is frequently used. The rule of trying to employ like sticking to identical measures should be adhered to in order to achieve a uniformity of sound.[4]

How to Tune. Tuning the drum is a vital aspect of percussion expertise and can be accomplished in the following manner: The *immediate area* by each screw should be tapped lightly with a finger. If the area is *flat* the screw should be tightened, and if the area is *sharp* the screw should be loosened. It is sometimes helpful to hold a finger in the middle of the drum during the tuning process. Ideally, both heads should be tuned to the same pitch in order to achieve the best results. The tuning process is essentially the same for all drums. It should be noted that many students have a tendency to play on drumheads that are too loose. Since a fairly crisp sound is usually desired from the snare drum, its head should be kept relatively tight at all times.

A selected list of drum solo literature for the development of individual skills

It is hoped that this graded list of available publications will be helpful to the instructor in developing his students for the high school band. If the student's musical growth is to be considered along with his technical development, attention must be given to the quality of music studied and performed. The following list was selected from a great deal of available literature. An effort was made to include material perhaps less well known in addition to many of the standard works. When grading this literature, the musical as well as the technical difficulty was taken into consideration. It should be noted, however, that the grading is arbitrary and intended only to give a general classification concerning the musical and technical difficulty. The grading ranges from "easy" through "difficult."

Able, "Hi Ho Simpson." Fillmore (Difficult)
Benson, "Three Dances." Chappell (Moderately Difficult)
Berg, "Festival Capers." Bourne (Difficult)
Buchtel, "Drumnastics." Kjos (Easy)
Buggert, "Bobbin' Back." Rubank (Moderately Difficult)
Buggert, "Echoing Sticks." Rubank (Moderately Difficult)
Buggert, "Meteorite." Belwin (Moderately Easy)

---

[4] Jerry Kent, *Handbook for the School Drummer* (Denver, Colorado: Jerry Kent, 1964), pp. 23–26.

Buggert, "Thundering Through." Rubank (Moderately Difficult)

Cappio, "Primo." Ludwig (Moderately Difficult)

Christian, "Strollin'." Ludwig (Moderately Difficult)

Colgrass, "Six Unaccompanied Solos." G. Schirmer (Moderately Easy)

Collins, "The Badger Strut." Ludwig (Moderately Easy)

Epperson, "Dick C. Doodle." Carl Fischer (Easy)

Goldenberg, "A Little Suite for Snare Drum." Shapiro-Bernstein (Moderately Difficult)

Harr, "Carolyn." Cole (Easy)

Harr, "Jombo's Holiday." (Bass Drum) Rubank (Moderately Easy)

Harr, "Mr. Boom-Boom." (Bass Drum) Rubank (Moderately Easy)

Harr, "The Twenty-Six." Cole (Difficult)

Harris, "The Solo Drummer." (Compilation) F. Colombo (Moderately Easy to Moderately Difficult)

Heney, "American Patrol." Rubank (Moderately Easy)

Heney, "General Grant." Fillmore (Difficult)

Heney, "General Pershing." Fillmore (Moderately Difficult)

Kelly, "Newfulf Drummer." Rubank (Moderately Easy)

Markovich, "Countdown." Ludwig (Easy)

Markovich, "High Flyer." Ludwig (Easy)

Markovich, "Stamina." Ludwig (Difficult)

Markovich, "The Winner." Ludwig (Moderately Easy)

Markovich, "Tornado." Ludwig (Difficult)

Mitchell, "Forensic Taps." Kjos (Difficult)

Mitchell, "Forreest Capers." Kjos (Difficult)

Mitchell, "Rumbling Drums." Kjos (Moderately Difficult)

Ostling, "First Competition." Music Publishers Holding Corporation (Easy)

Ostling, "Rudimental Review." Music Publishers Holding Corporation (Difficult)

Prentice, "Pass in Review." Belwin (Moderately Difficult)

Prentice, "Toyland Parade." Belwin (Easy)

Price, "Exhibition Drum Solo No. 1." Music for Percussion (Difficult)

Rackett, "High School Drummer." Rubank (Moderately Difficult)

Schinstine, "By the River." Southern (Easy)

Schinstine, "Rudimental Rondo." Southern (Moderately Difficult)

Stone, "Scholastic Six-Eight." Stone (Moderately Difficult)

Stone, "Yours Rudimentally." Stone (Difficult)

Street, "Swinging Down the Street." (with Bass Drum and Cymbals) Fillmore (Difficult)

Thamm, "Etude in Accents." Ludwig (Easy)

Selected bibliography

Blades, James, *Orchestral Percussion Technique.* London. Oxford University Press, 1961.

Baldwin, John, "A Gripping Topic: To Match or Not to Match," *The School Musician,* vol. 39, August-September, 1967, p. 18.

Bartlett, Harry R., *Guide to Teaching Percussion.* Dubuque, Iowa: Wm. C. Brown Company, 1964.

Beck, John H., "A Complete Listing of All NACWPI Percussion Articles," *National Association of College Wind and Percussion Instructors Bulletin,* vol. 14, Summer, 1966, p. 22.

Berryman, Joe, "Percussion" in *Building Better Bands.* Rockville Centre, L.I., New York: Belwin, Inc., 1957.

Collins, Myron D. and John E. Green, *Playing and Teaching Percussion Instruments.* Englewood Cliffs, New Jersey: Prentice-Hall, Inc., 1962.

Fink, Ron, "Tips on Contest Snare Drumming," *The Instrumentalist,* vol. 17, April, 1963, p. 83.

How to Care for Your Instrument. Elkhart, Indiana: C. G. Conn, Ltd., 1942.

Kent, Jerry, *Handbook for the School Drummer.* Denver, Colorado: Jerry Kent, 1964.

McKenzie, Jack and H. Payson, *Music Educator's Guide to Percussion.* Rockville Centre, L.I., New York: Belwin, Inc., 1964.

Peters, Gordon B., *Treatise on Percussion* (Unpublished Master's Thesis, Eastman School of Music of the University of Rochester), 1962.

Salmon, James D., "Membranophones and Idiophones—Mallets, Sticks, and Beaters," *National Association of College Wind and Percussion Instructors Bulletin,* vol. 12, October, 1963, p. 16.

Sewrey, James, "Percussion Instruction: What to Do," *The School Musician,* vol. 37, May, 1966, p. 22.

Spohn, Charles L., *The Percussion.* Boston, Mass.: Allyn and Bacon, Inc., 1967.

White, Charles L., *Drums Through the Ages.* Los Angeles, California: Sterling Press, 1960.

CHAPTER 17

The Bass Drum and Cymbals, Timpani, and Mallet Instruments

The bass drum, cymbals, and timpani have long been recognized as essential to the instrumentation of the band. In addition, most high school bands also use a number of the so-called mallet instruments. These include the xylophone, bells and bell lyra, chimes, marimba, and the vibraharp. Most aspiring percussion students should work to attain a degree of facility on a number of the percussion instruments. It is a rare case where an advanced percussionist will not possess this multiple facility. Actually, the percussionist should have at least some acquaintance with all of the percussion instruments. The challenge provided by these instruments can have a very salutary effect on the entire percussion section of the high school band.

Selecting instructional materials

Adequate instructional materials are available for these instruments. The following is a representative listing.

Beginning Methods and Supplementary Studies

Basic Method for the Drums (Snare Drum, Bass Drum, Cymbals, and Traps) Berryman .... Carl Fischer

Elementary Methods for Marimba-Xylophone, Timpani,
and Bell Lyra (separate books) .... Rubank
Modern Method (Gardner) .... Carl Fischer
    Part 1, Drums, Cymbals, Accessories
    Part 2, Bells, Xylophone, Vibraphone
    Part 3, Timpani
Foundation Studies for Vibes, Xylophone or Marimba
(Gornston) .... David Gornston
Ludwig Timpani Instructor (Ludwig) .... Ludwig
Xylophone and Marimba Method, Volume I
(Schaefer) .... Henry Adler

Intermediate Methods and Supplementary Studies

Foot Cymbal and Bass Drum Control (Gornston) .... Sam Fox
The Art of Playing Cymbals (Denov) .... Adler
Mallet Technique for Xylophone, Marimba, and
Vibraphone (Firth) .... Carl Fischer
Modern Method for Timpani (Goodman) .... Mills
Intermediate Methods for Marimba, Xylophone, Vibes
(Separate Books) .... Rubank
Modern School for the Xylophone, Marimba, Vibraphone
(Goldenberg) .... Chappell
Practical Method of Developing Finger Control
(Burns-Malin) .... Henry Adler

Advanced Methods and Supplementary Studies

Timpani Method (Friese-Lepak) .... Henry Adler
New Method of Velocity for Xylophone, Marimba and
Vibraphone (Strelsin) .... Carl Fischer
Solo Timpanist (Firth) .... Carl Fischer
Mental and Manual Calisthenics for the Modern Mallet
Player (Bailey) .... Henry Adler

Choosing the instruments, student adaptability, recordings, and instrument care

In the case of the bass drum a double tension 16″ x 36″ instrument with plastic heads gives good results. The bass drummer should have *a minimum* of two beaters—the standard double-end lamb's wool beater and a hard felt-tip beater. A number of other beaters should also be available to make possible the achievement of various special effects on the bass drum.

Cymbals can be purchased in numerous sizes and thicknesses.

The standard model for the high school band is generally a medium-thickness, 18 inch instrument. A larger cymbal should be used for the marching band, and several smaller cymbals should also be included among the school's percussion equipment.

The best overall timpani for use in the high school band is probably the 25 inch and 28 inch set which can be *pedal-tuned* and has plastic heads. A number of timpani sticks should be available, ranging from very soft ones (which emphasize resonance) to wooden ones (for special percussive and rhythmic passages). Professional timpanists usually make their own sticks or have them made to their specifications.

Many of the mallet percussion instruments also represent major purchases. It should be remembered, however, that these instruments will usually outlast most any other instrument in the band, assuming that they receive proper care. High quality, first-line instruments are again the least expensive in the long run. Clearly, attention should be given to the quality of materials used in the instrument as well as to the craftsmanship involved in its construction. The mallet instruments should also be carefully checked for accurate intonation before they are purchased.

Since many of the percussion instruments represent considerable investments, the instrumental director who is not a percussion specialist would do well to solicit the advice and recommendations of an expert in this area when selecting and purchasing percussion instruments.

Rhythm is a vital factor to be taken into consideration when considering students for these percussion instruments. Other important factors include: innate musical talent, fine pitch sensitivity, good general intelligence and the student's enthusiasm toward the instrument. As always, a piano background is helpful. Physically, the student needs to have good wrist dexterity and flexibility.

The following are representative recordings which are available to the instructor and student as instructional aids:

"American Percussion Society," Paul Price, conductor. Urania record #UX-106.

"Percussion Performance," Mervin Britton, Percussionist. (features castanets, triangle, and tambourine) Available from Lyons Band Instrument Co.

"Percussion Music," Paul Price, conductor. Period record #743.

"Spotlight on Percussion," VOX record #DL 180.

"Ithaca Percussion Ensemble," Golden Crest record #4016.

Suggestions and recommendations for the care and storage of the percussion instruments are found in Chapter 16. Since many of these instruments are normally school-owned, it is wise for the director to inspect them carefully at regular intervals. Adequate storage space, proper temperature, and proper humidity all play key roles in helping these instruments to perform better, last longer, and cost less to maintain. Specific and detailed instructions regarding the care and maintenance of all major percussion instruments are readily available from any manufacturer.

Teaching the bass drum and cymbals, mallet instruments, and timpani

Three important aspects which the concert bass drummer needs to consider are his style, choice of mallets, and the muffling of the instrument. John Beck indicates: "Marches sound best when the left hand is placed on the opposite head from the beating head. Show tunes sound best when the left hand is placed on the opposite head and the right knee is on the beating head."[1] The choice of mallet also affects the style. The bass drummer should have three mallets available to him. These include a hard felt mallet, two timpani mallets, and the usual lamb's wool mallet.

The Bass Drum. Tuning the bass drum is actually more important than many realize. The beating head of the bass drum should be looser than its opposite head. This will produce a sound which has *impact* caused by the looseness of the beating head. This sound will also have *resonance* caused by the tighter opposite head. The bass drum should not be tuned to a definite pitch and its sound should not have a great deal of ring.[2]

Striking the bass drum in the proper place is essential if good results are to be achieved. This should normally be from six to eight inches from the rim of the instrument and from four to six inches away from the center of the head. The exact location of

---

[1]John H. Beck, "Bass Drum and Cymbals," *National Association of College Wind and Percussion Instructors Bulletin*, Fall, 1966, p. 3.

[2]*Ibid.*, p. 4.

the striking point will, of course, vary according to the style of the composition being performed. The bass drum stick should be held in essentially the same manner as the right hand snare drum stick. (See Figure 17-A.) Good tone production is also an important aspect of bass drum playing. This depends very much

Figure 17–A Note the bass drum beater is gripped in much the same manner as the right snare drum stick. The bass drum tone is best when the drum is struck from four to six inches away from the center of the head and six to eight inches from the rim of the instrument

upon the way the drum is struck. The sound should be *drawn out* of the drum by making use of the arm as well as the wrist.

The Cymbals. Every percussion student should be familiar with the proper way to perform on the cymbals. When crashing these instruments the left hand should be held still while the right cymbal is moved upward. The cymbals should be struck a *glancing* blow approximately three inches below the top of the left cymbal in order to avoid the "airlock." The crash should be completed by following through and then holding the cymbals at arm's length in order to achieve maximum vibration. The sides of the body or chest can be used to dampen the crash.[3] Most authorities prefer leather thongs for holding the cymbals. Since cymbals are normally "paired" at the factory it is recommended that they be purchased in pairs. Selecting and matching cymbals properly requires a great deal of skill and professional expertise.

Mallet Instruments. All mallet percussion instruments are played with basically the same technique.[4] Correct playing habits should, of course, be introduced in the early grades. Students should not be allowed to play the marimba, vibes, or xylophone with one hand. The director should also not allow one-handed bell playing except on the bell lyra in the marching band. Two mallets should even be used when playing the chimes.[5] These percussion instruments have numerous kinds of mallets which are used for different effects or for playing in the various registers of the instruments. Many composers now indicate specifically the type of mallet they want used. The different types of mallets should be made available for use by the high school percussionist. Their detailed description and function is available from any manufacturer of percussion instruments and percussion equipment.

The Timpani. Most timpani players have been first trained in the fundamentals of snare drumming. Unlike snare drumming, a major aspect of timpani performance presupposes that the player have a good ear. This is a necessity. The timpani sticks should be held in the following two manners (See Figures 17-B and 17-C):

---

[3]Vernon F. Leidig, *Contemporary Percussion Technique and Method* (Hollywood: Highland Music Company, 1960), p. 11.

[4]Wallace Barnett, *The Mallet Percussions and How to Use Them* (Chicago: J. C. Deagan, Inc., 1968), p. 11.

[5]*Ibid.*

Figure 17–B   Playing Position for the Tympani
Note that the sticks are held with the thumb and forefinger gripping them, thus allowing the butt ends to rest in the palm of the hand similar to the right hand snare drum grip

1. Both sticks held in the position of the right hand snare drum stick with the tops of the hands being visible.
2. Both sticks held in the right hand snare drum position with the thumbs on *top* instead of at the side.

Both of these positions are frequently employed. Many perform-

Figure 17–C   Muffling the Tympani
**An important aspect of tympani playing is the muffling of the
drum. Proper muffling is accomplished by the last three fingers
of the hand being pressed firmly but lightly against the head**

ers use these two positions according to the effects required in
the composition being played.

Proper tuning is, of course, very important. The student should
begin to learn to tune the timpani as early as possible in his
studies. It is a good idea to use timpani which *do not* have tuning

gauges for the purpose of this training. Ideally, the student should be able to tune the instruments *without any aids*. This is where ear training becomes important. The student should become familiar with intervals and intervallic interrelationships, thus making him able to tune the timpani effectively in any situation.

Much time should be spent in getting the student to set the heads of the timpani in motion properly. The sound should again be *drawn out* of the instrument and not beat into it, unless specifically called for in the music. A good deal of time also needs to be spent in developing the roll and its variations. A number of different kinds of mallets should be available for use by the timpanist in order to achieve different effects called for in the music. The student timpanist should also do much sight-reading with as many tuning situations as possible.

PERCUSSION INSTRUMENT NAMES BY LANGUAGES

English	Italian	German	French
Bass Drum	Gran Cassa	Grosse Trommel	Crosse Caisse
Bells	Campanelle	Glocken	Cloches
Castanets	Castagnette	Kastagnetten	Castagnettes
Celesta	Celesta	Celeste	Celeste
Chimes	Campane	Glocken	Cloches
Cymbals	Piatti or Cinelli	Becken	Cymbals
Glockenspiel	Campanetta	Glockenspiel	Carillon
Gong	Tam-Tam	Tam-Tam	Tam-Tam
Marimba	Marimba	Marimba	Marimba
Snare Drum	Tamburo Militare	Kleine Trommel	Tambour Militaire
Tambourine	Tamburino	Schellentrommel	Tambour de Basque
Tenor Drum	Tambouro rullante	Ruhrtrommel	Caisse roulante
Timpani	Timpani	Pauken	Timbales
Triangle	Triangolo	Triangel	Triangle
Xylophone	Zilafone	Xylophone	Xylaphone

A selected list of solo literature for the development of individual skills

It is hoped that this graded list of available publications will be helpful to the instructor in terms of developing his students for the high school band. If the student's musical growth is to be taken into consideration in addition to his technical development, attention must be given to the quality of music studied and per-

formed. The following list was selected from a great deal of literature now available for these instruments. The technical difficulty
of the literature was taken into consideration when grading it.
The grading is, however, arbitrary and intended to assign only a
general classification regarding both the musical as well as the
technical difficulty. The grading ranges from "easy" through
"difficult."

MARIMBA, VIBRAHARP AND XYLOPHONE

Anderson, "Fiddle Faddle." Mills (Moderately Easy)

Brahms-Quick, "Hungarian Dance #5." Rubank (Easy)

Breuer, "Improvisation #1 for Vibes." Gornston (Moderately Easy)

Creston, "Concerto for Marimba and Orchestra." (Piano reduction
available). G. Schirmer (Difficult)

De Gastyne, "Prelude #3 for Vibraharp." Fereol (Difficult)

Delibes-Edwards, "Sylvia." Rubank (Moderately Easy)

Dinicu-Heifetz, "Hora Staccato." Carl Fischer (Difficult)

Dorn, (arr.) "Solos for Marimba, Vibes, and Xylophone." Adler (Easy
to Moderately Difficult)

Dreves, "Latin Bells." (Bell Solo) Belwin (Easy)

Dvorak-Quick, "Largo" from the *New World Symphony* Rubank
(Moderately Easy)

Frazeur, "The Quiet Place." Kendor (Easy)

Garrison-Zoller, "Raindrops." Alfred (Moderately Easy)

Green, "Caprice Valsant." Carl Fischer (Moderately Difficult)

Green, "Valse Brillante." Carl Fischer (Difficult)

Haydn-Breuer, "Allegro." Carl Fischer (Easy)

Heney, (arr.) "Carnival of Venice." Fillmore (Difficult)

Jolliff, (arr.) "Music for the Marimba." Rubank. Volumes I, II, and
III. (Easy to Moderately Difficult)

Jolliff, (arr.) "78 Solos for Marimba." Belwin (Easy to Moderately
Difficult)

Kabalevsky-Goldenberg, "The Galloping Comedians." Leeds (Difficult)

Milhaud, "Concerto for Marimba, Vibes, and Orchestra." (Piano reduction available). Associated (Moderately Difficult)

Musser, "Prelude." Music Publishers Holding Corporation (Moderately
Easy)

Owen, "Chopsticks." Fillmore (Moderately Easy)

Porter-Klickman, "Begin the Beguine." Harms (Moderately Easy)

Rogers, "Mirage." Southern (Moderately Easy)

Schubert-Edwards, "Ave Maria." Rubank (Easy)

Shostakovich-Maganini, "Polka" from *The Golden Age* Edition Musicus (Difficult)

Thomas-Luscomb, "Raymond Overture." Rubank (Moderately Difficult)

Thomas-Wallace, "Entr'acte Gavotte" from *Mignon* Carl Fischer (Moderately Difficult)

Tschaikowsky-Dreves, "Waltz of the Flowers." (Bell Solo) Belwin (Easy)

Weber-Sifert, "Invitation to the Waltz." Belwin (Difficult)

TIMPANI

Britton, "Solo Piece for Timpani." Music for Percussion (Moderately Easy)

Goodman, "Ballad for the Dance." Mills (Difficult)

Harr, "Bunker Hill." Cole (Moderately Difficult)

McKenzie, "Six Graded Solos." Music for Percussion (Moderately Easy)

Muczynski, "Three Designs for Three Timpani." G. Schirmer (Moderately Difficult)

Noak, "Suite for Timpani." Music for Percussion (Moderately Difficult)

Price, "Solos for Timpani." Music for Percussion (Moderately Easy to Difficult)

Schinstine, "Tall Tale for Timpani." Southern (Easy)

Schinstine, "Timpendium." Southern (Difficult)

Tcherepnine, "Sonatina for Timpani." Boosey & Hawkes (Moderately Difficult)

Selected bibliography

Blades, James, *Orchestral Percussion Technique*. London: Oxford University Press, 1961.

Barnett, Wallace, "The Mallet Percussions," *The Instrumentalist*, vol. 17, December, 1962, p. 65.

Barnett, Wallace, *The Mallet Percussions and How to Use Them.* Chicago, Illinois: J. C. Deagan, Inc., 1968.

Bartlett, Harry R., *Guide to Teaching Percussion.* Dubuque, Iowa: Wm. C. Brown Company, 1964.

Beck, John H., "Bass Drum and Cymbals," *National Association of College Wind and Percussion Instructors Bulletin*, vol. 15, Fall, 1966, p. 2.

Beck, John H., "A Complete Listing of All NACWPI Percussion Articles," *National Association of College Wind and Percussion Instructors Bulletin*, vol. 14, Summer, 1966, p. 22.

Berryman, Joe, "Percussion" in *Building Better Bands.* Rockville Centre, L.I., New York: Belwin, Inc., 1957.

Collins, Myron D. and John E. Green, *Playing and Teaching Percussion Instruments.* Englewood Cliffs, New Jersey: Prentice-Hall, Inc., 1962.

Denov, Sam, *The Art of Playing the Cymbals.* New York, New York: Henry Adler, Inc., 1963.

How to Care for Your Instrument. Elkhart, Indiana: C. G. Conn, Ltd., 1942.

Kent, Jerry, *Handbook for the School Drummer.* Denver, Colorado: Jerry Kent, 1964.

Leidig, Vernon F., *Contemporary Percussion Technique and Method.* Hollywood, California: Highland Music Co., 1960.

McCormick, Larry, "Effective Use of Cymbals," *The Instrumentalist*, vol. 22, October, 1967, p. 75.

McKenzie, Jack and H. Payson, *Music Educator's Guide to Percussion.* Rockville Centre, L.I., New York: Belwin, Inc., 1964.

Masoner, Betty, "The Bass Drummer," *The Instrumentalist*, vol. 17, April, 1963, p. 83.

Noonan, John, *Notes on Striking Cymbals.* North Quincy Mass.: Avedis Zildqian Co., 1962.

Peters, Gordon B., "Marimba in the Concert Band," *The Instrumentalist*, vol. 17, October, 1962, p. 75.

Peters, Gordon B., *Treatise on Percussion* (Unpublished Master's Thesis, Eastman School of Music of the University of Rochester), 1962.

Salmon, James D., "Membranophones and Idiophones—Mallets, Sticks, and Beaters," *National Association of College Wind and Percussion Instructors Bulletin*, vol. 12, October, 1963, p. 16.

Spohn, Charles L., *The Percussion*. Boston, Massachusetts: Allyn and Bacon Inc., 1967.

White, Charles L., *Drums Through the Ages*. Los Angeles, California: Sterling Press, 1960.

General

Baines, A., *Woodwind Instruments and Their History*. W. W. Norton, 1957.

Brand, E., *Band Instrument Repair Manual*. Eric Brand, 1946.

Buchner, H., *Musical Instruments Through the Ages*. McGinnis & Marx, 1949.

Cahn, M., *The Instrumentalist's Handbook and Dictionary*. Forman, 1958.

Duvall, W., *The High School Band Director's Handbook*. Prentice-Hall, 1960.

Farkas, P., *The Art of Brass Playing*. Brass Publications, 1962.

Galpin, Francis, *A Textbook of European Musical Instruments*. J. De-Graff, 1956.

Geiringer, K., *Musical Instruments: Their History in Western Culture*. Oxford, 1945.

Globus, Rudo S., *The Woodwind Anthology*. McGinnis & Marx, 1952.

Helm, Sanford, *Catalogue of Chamber Music for Wind Instruments*. McGinnis & Marx, 1952.

Hendrickson, Clarence V., *Fingering Charts for Instrumentalists*. Carl Fischer, 1958.

Holz, Emil A. and Roger Jacobi, *Teaching Band Instruments to Beginners*. Prentice-Hall, 1966.

House, R., *Instrumental Music for Today's Schools*. Prentice-Hall, 1965.

Hunt, Norman, *A Guide to Teaching Brass*. Wm. Brown, 1968.

Kuhn, W., *Instrumental Music*. Allyn & Bacon, 1962.

Langwill, Lyndesay G., *An Index of Musical Wind Instrument Makers*. McGinnis & Marx, 1963.

Neidig, Kenneth L., *The Band Director's Guide*. Prentice-Hall, 1964.

Porter, Maurice M., *The Embouchure*. Boosey & Hawkes, 1967.

Rasmussen, Mary, *A Teacher's Guide to the Literature of Brass Instruments*. Brass Quarterly, 1964.

Rasmussen, Mary and Donald Mattran, *A Teacher's Guide to the Literature of Woodwind Instruments*. Appleyard Publishing Co., 1966.

Sachs, C., *The History of Musical Instruments*. W. W. Norton, 1940.

Sachs, C., *Woodwind Anthology*. Woodwind Magazine, McGinnis & Marx, 1952.

Schwartz, Harry W., *The Story of Musical Instruments*. Doubleday, 1938.

Snyder, Keith D., *School Music Administration and Supervision*. Allyn & Bacon, 1965.

Tiede, Clayton H., *The Practical Band Instrument Repair Manual*. Wm. C. Brown, 1962.

Timm, E., *The Woodwinds*. Allyn & Bacon, 1964.

Weyland, Rudolph, *A Guide to Effective Music Supervision*. Wm. Brown, 1968.

Westphal, F., *Guide to Teaching Woodwinds*. Wm. C. Brown, 1962.

Winslow, Robert W. and John E. Green, *Playing and Teaching Brass Instruments*. Prentice-Hall, 1961.

Winter, James H., *The Brass Instruments*. Allyn & Bacon, 1964.

Wyand, Alan, *Band Training Camps*. Alan Wyand, 1962.

Clarinet and Saxophone

Bonade, D., *Clarinetist's Compendium*. Leblanc Publications, 1956.

Cailliet, Lucien, *The Clarinet and Clarinet Choir*. Leblanc Publications, 1955.

Eby, W., *The Clarinet Embouchure*. Walter Jacobs, 1927.

Eby, W., *The Saxophone Embouchure*. McGinnis & Marx, 1946.

Heim, Norman M., *A Handbook for Clarinet Performance*. Norman Heim, U. of Maryland, 1966.

McCathren, D., *Playing and Teaching the Clarinet Family*. Southern Music, 1959.

Opperman, K., *Repertory of the Clarinet*. G. Ricordi, 1960.

Pace, Kenneth L., *Handbook of Clarinet Playing*. Dehoff Publications, 1967.

Reed, A., *The Balanced Clarinet Choir*. G. Leblanc Corp., 1958.

Rendall, F., *The Clarinet: Some Notes upon its History and Construction*. Philosophical Library, 1954.

Stein, K., *The Art of Clarinet Playing*. Summy-Bichard, 1958.

Stubbins, W. H., *The Art of Clarinetistry*. Ann Arbor Publishers, 1965.

Teal, L., *The Art of Saxophone Playing*. Summy-Birchard, 1963.

Thurston, F., *Clarinet Technique*. Oxford, 1956.

Tosè, G., *Artistic Clarinet Technique and Study*. Highland Music Co., 1962.

Willaman, R., *The Clarinet and Clarinet Playing*. Carl Fischer, 1949.

Oboe

Bate, P., *The Oboe: An Outline of its History, Development and Construction*. Ernest Benn, 1956.

Organ, Robert J., *The Oboe, Performance and Teaching*. Rebo, 1954.

Rothwell, Evelyn, *Oboe Technique*. Oxford, 1953.

Russell, Myron E., *Oboe Reed Making and Problems of the Oboe Player*. Jack Spratt, 1963.

Sprenkle, R., & D. Ledet, *The Art of Oboe Playing*. Summy-Birchard, 1961.

Bassoon

Camden, Archie, *Bassoon Technique*. Oxford University Press, 1962.

Fox, Hugo, *Let's Play Bassoon*. Fox Bassoon Co., 1963.

Heckle, W., *The Bassoon*. Jack Spratt, 1940.

Langwill, L., *The Bassoon and Double Bassoon*. Hinrichen Edition, 1948.

Organ, Robert J., *The Bassoon, Performance and Teaching*. Rebo, 1954.

Risdon, Howard, *Musical Literature for the Bassoon*. Berdon, Inc., 1963.

Spencer, William, *The Art of Bassoon Playing*. Summy-Birchard, 1958.

Flute

Boehm, T., *The Flute and Flute Playing*. McGinnis & Marx, 1960.

Chapman, F., *Flute Technique*. Oxford, 1958.

DeLorenzo, L., *My Complete Story of the Flute*. Citadel Press, 1951.

Fitzgibbon, H., *The Story of the Flute*. Charles Scribner's Sons, 1914.

Kincaid, William and Claire Polin, *The Art and Practice of Modern Flute Technique*. Music Critics Assn., 1968.

Pellerite, J., *A Handbook of Literature for the Flute.* Zalo Publications, 1965.

Pellerite, J., *A Modern Guide to Fingerings for the Flute.* Zalo Publica-
Wilkins, F., *The Flutist's Guide.* F. Wilkins, 1957.
tions, 1964.

Reeds

Artley, Joe, *How to Make Double-Reeds for Oboe, English Horn, and Bassoon.* Jack Spratt, 1953.

Mayer, R., & T. Rohner, *Oboe Reeds: How to Make and Adjust Them. The Instrumentalist,* 1953.

Opperman, K., *Handbook for Making and Adjusting Single Reeds.* Chappell, 1956.

Spratt, Jack, *How to Make Your Own Clarinet Reeds.* Jack Spratt, 1956.

Acoustics

Bartholomew, W., *Acoustics of Music.* Prentice-Hall, 1942.

Benade, A., *Horns, Strings and Harmony—The Science of Enjoyable Sounds.* Anchor Books, Doubleday, 1960.

Culver, C., *Musical Acoustics.* McGraw-Hill, 1956.

Jeans, James, *Science and Music.* Macmillan, 1939.

Pottle, Ralph, *Tuning the School Band and Orchestra.* Southeastern Louisiana State College (Hammond, La.), 1962.

Richardson, G., *Acoustics of Orchestral Instruments and the Organ.* Edward Arnold, 1929.

Stauffer, D., *Intonation Deficiencies of Wind Instruments in Ensemble.* Catholic University of America Press, 1954.

Trumpet

Bate, Philip, *The Trumpet and Trombone.* W. W. Norton & Co., Inc., 1966.

Bush, Irving R., *Artistic Trumpet Technique and Study.* Highland Music Co., 1962.

Dale, D., *Trumpet Technique.* Oxford, 1965.

Gibson, Daryl J., *A Textbook for Trumpet.* T. S. Denison & Company, Inc., 1962.

Hanson, Fay, *Brass Playing, the Mechanism and the Technic.* Carl Fischer, Inc., 1968.

Noble, Clyde E., *The Psychology of Cornet and Trumpet Playing.* Montana State University Press, 1964.

Weast, Robert D., *Brass Performance*. McGinnis & Marx, 1962.

French Horn

Farkas, Philip, *The Art of French Horn Playing*. Summy-Birchard, 1956.

Gregory, Robin, *The Horn*. Faber and Faber, 1961.

Schuller, Gunther, *Horn Technique*. Oxford, 1962.

Trombone & Baritone

Bate, Philip, *The Trumpet and Trombone*. W. W. Norton & Company, Inc., 1966.

Kleinhammer, Edward, *The Art of Trombone Playing*. Summy-Birchard Co., 1962.

Tuba

Bell, William J., *A Handbook of Information on Intonation*. The Getzen Co., Inc., 1965.

Percussion

Bailey, Elden C., *Mental and Manual Calisthenics for the Modern Mallet Player*. Henry Adler, 1963.

Barnett, Wallace, *The Mallet Percussions and How to Use Them*. J. C. Deagan, Inc., 1964.

Bartlett, Harry R., *Guide to Teaching Percussion*. Wm. C. Brown Co., 1964.

Blades, James, *Orchestral Percussion Technique*. Oxford, 1961.

Collins, Myron D. and John E. Green, *Playing and Teaching Percussion Instruments*. Prentice-Hall, Inc., 1962.

Denov, Sam, *The Art of Playing the Cymbals*. Henry Adler, Inc., 1963.

McKenzie, Jack and A. Payson, *Music Educator's Guide to Percussion*. Belwin, Inc., 1964.

Noonan, John, *Notes on Striking Cymbals*. Avedis Zildjian Co., 1962.

Peters, Gordon B., *Treatise on Percussion*. (Unpublished Master's Thesis, Eastman School of Music of the University of Rochester), 1962.

Spohn, Charles L., *The Percussion*. Allyn & Bacon Inc., 1967.

Taylor, Henry W., *The Art and Science of the Timpani*. Dufour, 1964.

White, Charles L., *Drums Through the Ages*. Sterling Press, 1960.

Encyclopedias and Dictionaries

Apel, Willi, *Harvard Dictionary of Music.* Harvard University Press, 1945.

Baker's Biographical Dictionary of Musicians. G. Schirmer, 1940.

Baker, T., *Dictionary of Musical Terms.* G. Schirmer, 1939.

Barlow and Morgenstern, *A Dictionary of Musical Themes.* Crown Publishers, 1948.

Elson's Music Dictionary. Oliver Ditson Co., 1906.

Ewen, David, *Living Musicians.* H. H. Wilson Co., 1940.

Grove's Dictionary of Music and Musicians, Macmillan Co., 1940.

Hughes, Rupert, *Biographical Dictionary of Musicians.* Blue Ribbon Books, Inc., 1940.

Hughes, Rupert, *Music Lover's Encyclopedia.* Garden City Publishing Co., Inc., 1939.

Parkhurst and de Bekker, *Encyclopedia of Music and Musicians.* Crown Publishers, 1937.

Pratt, W. S., *The New Encyclopedia of Music and Musicians.* Macmillan Co., 1946.

Scholes, Percy, *Oxford Companion to Music.* Oxford University Press, 1947.

Thompson, Oscar, *The International Cyclopedia of Music and Musicians.* Dodd, Mead and Co., 1946.

Index

229